Willing to
DIE

ADVANCE PRAISE OF WILLING TO DIE

The story of this Romanian family is both engaging and intriguing! They have first-hand knowledge and experience of the evils from dictatorial Socialism and Communism. This is where America is now headed if we do not curb the onslaught of this vicious political philosophy that has crushed the lives and hopes of millions of God's children for so many decades. History is about to repeat itself as America bows to socialist ideologies and agendas under the guise of "Progressiveness." This nation must wake up and learn from those who know about and have experienced the dark side of this evil ideology. America is still the last bastion of hope for freedom, true prosperity and must continue to be the fortress for religious liberties from which our country sprang.

Harold Skousen
son of W. Cleon Skousen & President of Ensign Publishing
(W. Cleon Skousen, author of *New York Times* best seller *The Naked Communist*
and *New York Times* best seller *The Five Thousand Year Leap*)
Skousen2000.com

I first met the Muntean family in the late 1980's when ministering for Pastor Floyd Lawhon in Orange County, California. During the four week revival I became acquainted with this family from Romania, and their astonishing story of living under a Communist dictator and their amazing immigration to the United States. This book is a very intriguing true story that narrates a journey of destiny, proving the faithfulness of God during the most adverse circumstances. As an added note, when Jentezen Franklin and myself traveled to Romania to conduct a city-wide evangelistic meeting, the son of John, served as our interpreter through the trip, where hundreds under former communist chains, received Christ and were won to the Kingdom of God.

Perry Stone, Jr.
President and Founder of Voice of Evangelism Ministries

When John Muntean is willing to tell his story openly and transparently it is a great opportunity to listen, observe, and learn lessons for our own journey. I encourage you to do just that through this book.

Jentezen Franklin
Senior Pastor, Free Chapel, Author of *New York Times* best seller, *Fasting*

In the twelve to fourteen years I was their Pastor I watched them grow in this country but yet all the while they kept their deep devotions to their beloved Romania and raised their children to feel the same way.

I was privileged to watch him start with the shirt on his back and become a very model for the American dream.

I was also privileged to travel with John and Stela to his beloved Romania along with my precious wife. You can really learn much about someone by traveling with them. When we went to Romania, the country was still under the bondage of the tyrannical communist government of Nicolae and Elena Ceausescu and since John had become a US citizen it was amazing to see with one's own eyes the love and adoration with which his countrymen looked to him for leadership and guidance.

We traveled to the eastern bloc countries several times (about five or six if memory serves me right) and I watched John and Stela give of their time and money in abundance until when we started back home after two or three weeks he would literally be emotionally and physically exhausted.

Thank God for the lives of John and Stella Muntean. They are beautiful and Godly people and dearly beloved by the Lawhons.

Pastor Floyd Lawhon
Member of the World Mission for the Church of God
International Executive Council for Church of God, 1984-1988, 1990-1994, 1996-2000

Brother John with his wife, Stela, and their whole family are very dear to me, as only spiritual parents can be to a young man. They belong to a bygone generation; quiet and tender warriors, strong in faith and conviction, a people from another world . . .

Their life story is not only a story of survival, but it is one of faith and victory in the darkest of times. Living in communist Romania, under a brutal dictatorship, they faced the possibility of death every day. Still, they survived those times by trusting God and loving people unconditionally.

Their tale is like a breath of fresh air for the younger generations who often navigate between moral absolutes and the social imperatives of a postmodern world without a spiritual compass like the Muntean family had. *Willing to Die* provides such a compass. The Munteans leave us a legacy of hope, faith, and sacrifice—a journey about a willingness to live for God, and for Him alone. Theirs is a path which for many believers means a one-way ticket to martyrdom.

Romania's golden age ended too soon with the coming of World War II (WWII). Caught between the Axis Powers and the Allies, Romania did not have the time to recover from the war, being taken up by the red avalanche of Bolshevism. Starting with 1945, Moscow cast its long, icy shadow over the Carpathians and ushered the Stalinist era. Twenty years of ethnic cleansing ensued.

Intellectuals, entrepreneurs, students, scholars, artist, artisans, clergy, and virtually anyone of questionable origins were hunted, executed, or thrown in massive prison camps.

The Stalinist Era was a period in the Romanian history when the Communist Party was more or less led from Moscow under Joseph Stalin. When the party was an illegal underground, Jews and other minorities made up a large proportion of its members.

Yet, once it became the new establishment, its Jewish pioneers began to be seen as undeservedly and disproportionately privileged. From the late 1940s to the early 1960s a permanent purge ensued which replaced the community of Jewish veterans, wealthy business owners, brilliant intellectuals, community leaders, religious leaders, priests, pastors, and preachers who were labeled as potential "enemies of the state." They were not considered trustworthy—people of "questionable origins" who were a "non-patriotic group."

Thus, began the subtle killing of an entire generation. My father—a literature professor—was falsely accused of being against the regime and arrested. He was a community leader and school principal who refused to become a member of the Communist Party.

A case was staged in court, and in absence, he was condemned. Then, officials came to our home. In my presence, my father was taken to prison, leaving me with memories that haunt me to this day. He returned two years later when a 1964 general amnesty was granted.

After 1965, in response to mounting pressures from the West, the strategy had changed. In short, the entire country became a prison. Mistrust, fear, and constant surveillance under the auspices of the Securitate forces— Ceausescu's secret police—immersed into society's deep fabric in such a way it was impossible to know who was an enemy or a friend.

Brother turned against brother; spouses betrayed one another; parents spied on their children, and children became informants about their parents' activities. A toxicity of fear and suspicion seeped into the groundwater of everyday life. This familial and societal penetration was all possible because the very backbone of the country—the fathers of our generation—were destroyed in the prison camps, or, if they were lucky enough to survive, retreated into a life of loneliness and psychological despair.

Without strong leaders, a community crumbles. When communism collapsed on Christmas Day in December 1989, the nation found itself lead-erless and fatherless. For those of us who know the spiritual implications of fatherlessness, finding parents like the Munteans is, indeed, like finding a treasure.

They are among the few glimmering beacons of a generation that has largely sunk into obscurity. They are more than just people to be respected. They are living examples of God's love for us to follow.

People like them are alive today largely because many of them found an escape to the West. Here, they ironically fade from the memory of a genera-tion that only looks forward and very seldom back. This happened until Josephine Walker came along to commit to print their testimony in gripping detail with a strong sense of mission and responsibility.

Willing to Die is a story that needs to be read, applied, and never forgotten.

Pastor Ovidiu D. Druhora

1st Assistant Pastor, Emanuel Romanian Church of God

Anaheim, CA-USA

April 29, 2013

Willing to
DIE

THE TRUE STORY OF

JOHN MUNTEAN

as told to
Josephine Walker

AMBASSADOR INTERNATIONAL
GREENVILLE, SOUTH CAROLINA & BELFAST, NORTHERN IRELAND

www.ambassador-international.com

Willing To Die

ISBN: 978-1-62020-225-8
eISBN: 978-1-62020-323-1

Printed in the United States of America

Scripture quotations taken from the New American Standard Bible®,
Copyright © 1960, 1962, 1963, 1968, 1971, 1972, 1973,
1975, 1977, 1995 by The Lockman Foundation
Used by permission. (www.Lockman.org)

Interior photographs courtesy of the Muntean family

Cover art: Dabarti CGI and MarclSchauer / Shutterstock
Book design and typesetting: Matthew Mulder
E-book conversion: Anna Riebe

AMBASSADOR INTERNATIONAL
Emerald House
427 Wade Hampton Blvd.
Greenville, SC 29609, USA
www.ambassador-international.com

AMBASSADOR BOOKS
The Mount
2 Woodstock Link
Belfast, BT6 8DD, Northern Ireland, UK
www.ambassadormedia.co.uk

The colophon is a trademark of Ambassador

DEDICATION

I AM FOREVER GRATEFUL TO my father, Roman, and mother, Anica, for the strong foundation of faith and love they gave me. I will never forget the day my mother introduced me to my Lord, Jesus, nor her example of faith which she lived her entire life, and her continuous prayers for our safety.

With deep gratitude to my lovely wife of forty-nine years, Stela, who stood strong in faith by my side as we walked together on our journey. Thank you.

To my children: Ovidiu and his wife, Adriana; and their children Christina, Timothy, and Briana; Liviu and his wife, Lilly; my beautiful daughter, Tabita and her girls, Danielle and Karly; and my son, Daniel and his wife, Ana, along with Emily, Elijah, Luke, and Giana—I love and thank you for the joy you bring into my life. To secure your freedom from tyranny, I would do it all over again.

To God, thank You for guiding my life, and protecting me and my family while we lived under the horror of communism.

FURTHER ADVANCE PRAISE

When I first heard about John and Stela Muntean was in the mid-seventies. Radio Free Europe and The Voice Of America were broadcasting the action John Muntean of Sighisoara, Romania, was taking to secure his freedom. A teenager at those times, I was deeply impressed about the courage of such a man of God. It impressed me to the point of doing something similar or even more dramatic, if the work of God under Communism was to prosper in the Romania of those times. This was amplified by the truth that my own father and mother, respectively, Victor and Maria Gog were condemned and imprisoned by the communist authorities of Romania.

Mrs. Walker did a thorough and detailed job by taking her time to listen and pen the events of real people like the Munteans, and to put them in a written form for the generation to come after our times. Those reading this book are encouraged not to spend their Christian faith in self-complacency, neither in superficiality. Our walk with God is a real walk that involves action, a daily encounter with our Lord and Savior and making a living history with Him every day. This is the way Mrs. Walker managed to retell the story of John and Stela Muntean, whom I'm privileged to pastor and to call my loyal friends.

Rev. Dr. Lazar Gog
Emanuel Romanian Church of God, Senior Pastor, International Field Director
for the Church of God Romanian Office

TABLE OF CONTENTS

FOREWORD

SERVING THE LORD JESUS IS a privilege, not a reason to boast or be proud in the eyes of the world. What John and Stela Muntean, the Christian heroes of this fast-paced spiritual thriller, experienced under the oppressive system of Romania's Communist regime is not a distant true story, but a possible repetitive history.

The Church of the Living Savior, Jesus Christ, is a triumphant church, amidst many tribulations, persecutions, and oppositions from, in part, man and the devil. As the long waited Second Coming of our Lord and Savior draws near, the persecution and opposition of the world intensifies.

This truth, however, is not of the nature to discourage us, but to give us an impulse to become increasingly bold amid trials and tribulations. How are we going to do this?

There is no simple formula, neither one solution that fits all. However, there is a way to victory, power, and the manifestation of the presence of God—looking into the word of God, the life of Jesus, and the experience of the men and women of God like those in the pages of the Bible, or from the pages of church history.

In this thrilling book, the reader will re-live the power and freshness of God's Spirit through John and Stela Muntean's true story. I was a student when I first heard about the two heroes of this book. It came to my knowledge by the way of Radio Free Europe and the Voice of America.

The Christians of the free world did not comprehend the power of these two radio stations in oppressed countries like the Communist Romania of the seventies and eighties, when the story of this book took place. As a first generation student of an ever-approved seminary in Communist Romania, my life was deeply affected by what I have learned about the plea of the Munteans. I remembered my parents, imprisoned because of their faith, and I thought of what could await me in Christian ministry.

It takes faith and total dependence upon God and on our Lord and Savior, Jesus Christ, to live a true Christian life. It takes a complete reliance on God's Word and promises to be able to stand in Him, and be a real witness for His glorious kingdom. It takes a full surrender to the guidance of the Holy Spirit to walk straight through the labyrinth of Christianity daily trusting in Christ, our Lord and Mighty God.

The author of this book, Josephine Walker, was touched by such a living story as John's and Stela's. For the western Christian—who lives a life of plenty, freedom of speech, and expression—to read such a testimony might seem outside of human civilization. Yet, do not be deceived.

Last and this century are times when the Church of the Living God has experienced the harshest persecution and martyrdom. Yes, communism has fallen, but the threat and persecution against the church from the hand of militant and extremist Islam is without precedent.

The western church should not sleep the unwatchful sleep of self-complacency. With the trend of political correctness of today's society, a new turn in our religious freedom could start at any given time. This is why we should learn from the church's history and treasure the ever-truthfulness of the word of God.

So, travel with the Munteans and the author of the book into the not so distant past of the church. We learn to be prepared to give a true and faithful account of our life in Christ, no matter what lot in life will be cast upon us and our family.

Live the life of complete dependence upon Christ the Lord and the truth of His holy Word. The time is nearer to His Second Coming than we are prepared to think and believe. If we do not learn the history, it will repeat itself in a more devastating way for those weak in the faith than it was experienced years ago by our brothers and sisters in the faith, like John and Stela Muntean.

On the other hand, however, we must be prepared to make an even greater and braver history with our living Lord, Jesus than those who lived before us. The day of greatness for us in the faith is just around the corner. We must be ready, prepared, expectant, and confident in Him, Who is always with and for us. Christ Jesus is coming!

Dr. Lazar Gog
International Field Director, Church Of God Romanian Office
Anaheim, CA-USA
May 7, 2013

INTRODUCTION

HOW DOES A NATIVE-BORN WIDOW who hails from Cody, Wyoming, meet a transplanted Romanian couple from Costa Mesa, California when neither has visited the other's cities? They meet through their children, of course.

John and Stela's oldest son, Ovidiu, along with his wife and children, are great friends of my one and only daughter, Shannon, and her twin boys, Jarod and Jacob. On March 12, 2012, not quite a full four months after my husband passed away, my telephone rang. Ovidiu was on the other end and asked me if I would help his dad write his book.

That was the beginning of our journey—John and Stela Muntean, and me. One year later, at the end of March 2013, the manuscript for *Willing to Die* was emailed to the publisher. During that year, I interviewed John and Stela one hundred and six times.

They welcomed me as a guest into their home for three months. Our time together opened my eyes to see what true Communist persecution looks like. Even with all of that, it took a lot of research for me to fully grasp what Romanians suffered. Still, I only have a partial picture—twenty-three years after the revolution, the worst stories may not yet be told.

During the writing of this book we have laughed and cried, and then laughed and cried some more. We learned how close the three of us walk in spirit, our love for the Lord, and our country—and how much we fear for this nation.

Man's inhumanity toward man is something most Christians in the western world cannot fathom. In disbelief, we sit and listen until the tears fall and our minds and hearts say, "No more."

Many people simply do not want to hear the truth about what others have suffered in Communist countries. Yet, we must open our eyes and hearts to the truth—a life without God is capable of anything, I mean anything.

Even now, as I remember images I have seen and atrocities I have read about in research, my heart aches. Do not think it cannot happen here—it can, indeed.

John shared with me about his willingness to put his life on the line to get his family out of Romania. As I listened to his determination, I wondered if America still had men or women such as this—it used to. We still do.

Young and old, men and women, grandmas and grandpas are ready to stand strong against tyranny to preserve this amazing nation. However, there are not as many.

Unfortunately, there are those within and without who wish to destroy the America we once knew. This is not the America of my mother and father. It is not even the America I grew up in.

As I learned the Munteans' story and the truth about the destruction of a beautiful, productive country, I could not help, but see the parallels to America. The slow creeping of progressive socialism reminds me we usually only notice one ant at a time. We squish it, but another comes, and then another. We try to stop them, but they get into everything. Soon, they are everywhere. Progressive socialism is everywhere.

The idea behind socialism is as old as time. It has been ignored in the United States by most citizens until recent years. Now, there is nothing slow about its desire to devour our liberties.

The most important and exciting parts of John's and Stela's story were about how God used their enemies to bless them, and the many ways John's path was directed by the hand of God without him recognizing it at the time. Even living under those conditions, they experienced times of joy and happiness.

As you read the story, know this: our greatest desire is for God to be given the credit and glory for all He has done, and continues to do.

God does not work alone, as John's story proves.

If our great country is to be what it has been for over two hundred years, then we who love America have a lot of work to do, with God's help.

Josephine Walker

8:00 AM, OCTOBER 1977
BUCHAREST, ROMANIA

BLIZZARD-LIKE CONDITIONS, WITH HEAVY SNOW blowing sideways, made me almost invisible to the group of Romanian soldiers who guarded the American Embassy. I had already walked around the embassy looking for a way to slip past them.

The long black wool coat and furry Russian ushanka not only kept my head warm, but helped me blend in with the others on the street who rushed to work or hurried toward the bread lines. From across the street I studied the backside of the embassy.

There has to be a way inside without being stopped.

Some people might think me stupid to attempt this contact; however, without help my family had no hope. The living conditions under the brutal Communist leadership of Nicolae and Elena Ceausescu caused thousands to attempt escape. People took the chance, knowing—if caught—they faced possible imprisonment, torture, and even death.

Married couples lived with a bittersweet understanding and agreement. If a spouse was presented with the opportunity to escape, he or she would take it, leaving spouse and children behind to never know if or when they might be reunited. Until, and if, contact was made, fear and uncertainty ruled.

What drove people to take this risk? We lived in the prison known as Romania. Thirty-two years of communist rule brought the complete destruction of a country once called the Breadbasket of Europe.

Everywhere we went, we were watched. At work, in the schools, in the churches, and even on the streets informers looked and listened for something, anything to report. If they found nothing, lying was just as beneficial.

For years we lived with the extreme poverty, hard work and empty shelves, constant fear of the secret police, and the unending Communist control. How does a person live without hope or freedom? I could not, not any more.

Thousands before me had died seeking it. I had no intention of becoming one of them.

There had to be a way past the guards whose job it was to find out who I was, why I was there, and what business I had with the Americans.

I noticed many people dressed similar to me as they walked unhindered past the security guard at the back gate. They appeared to be employees.

With my briefcase in one hand, I flipped up my collar and pulled down the earflaps on my hat, and then quickly crossed the street. I passed through the gate pretending to be an employee.

Five feet from safety the guard yelled, "Stop!"

CHAPTER 1

DAYS ORDAINED

Thine eyes have seen my unformed substance; and in Thy
book they were all written, the days that were ordained for me,
when as yet there was not one of them.
—Psalm 139:16, NASB

"JOHN, YOU MUST UNDERSTAND, GIRLS don't like boys who don't know how to dance."

Early in my life, my sisters set their minds to teaching me as much as possible about the important things of life, and they made it clear dancing was one of them. At age five, my heart wanted nothing more than to please them.

My sister, Anica, older than me by two years, practiced all the popular folk dances of that time with me every night in our home. We became so skilled our older sisters took us to wherever the young people gathered for a time of singing and dancing.

I enjoyed dancing so much I even created my own. Surrounded by a circle of singing girls, I would twirl and slap my hands on the side of my boots. Then, I clicked my heels together, causing my spurs to jingle.

One dance, in particular, that lives in my memory required the male to speak a part while the female sang. Knowing it was important to perform it correctly, I worked hard to remember the words: "May God make all the girls like ewes and me a ram, so I can make lots of baby lambs."

When everyone broke out laughing—I had no idea why—I felt proud everyone seemed to like it. I was much older when I learned what it meant.

Life in our small village was peaceful and happy for me—the first seven years.

• • •

My name is Ioan (John) Muntean. I was born to Roman and Anica Muntean on October 29, 1938 in the village of Cergaul Mare, County of Alba, Transylvania, Romania. The sixth child, and only son among five sisters, meant I was a bit spoiled. I admit it, I was.

Our village, Cergaul Mare, was not considered large at all and had no paved roads, only dirt which often turned to deep ruts of mud in the fall and winters. With no electricity or indoor plumbing, we used kerosene lanterns and hauled water from the well.

The only store in the village offered a variety of products: tools, and food items. Large vegetable gardens along with apple and plum trees filled backyards and provided much of the needed food. After harvest, the wheat went to the granary for milling into flour.

Each family had livestock of horses, cows, pigs, sheep, chickens, and geese. Some folks used buffalo in place of oxen. What we did not produce, we bought at the swap meets in the city of Blaj. When we needed something not available in the village, once a week during the summer we walked or rode in the wagon eight miles to Blaj—winters, seldom.

All the homes in our village, if seen from above, would have looked similar with their bright red tile roofs. Our village was like a jigsaw puzzle, divided by a small creek and usually dry in the summer and fall. The three hundred and fifty homes sat on a plot of land about fifty acres in size, except with different dimensions. The standard two-room houses were painted different shades of blue, each had buildings behind them—the smaller summer kitchen, storage buildings, and a barn.

Our two-room home was no different; the larger of the two had a kitchen, a dining area, and space for a few chairs. The big woodstove in the kitchen, used for cooking meals in the cooler seasons, also provided our only heat in the bitter cold winters. Wardrobes filled with clothes lined one wall.

The second room doubled as a bedroom. My parents slept on the only bed while the rest of the family—five sisters and me—slept on benches which converted into a bed. The design of the bench/bed proved quite clever.

Each evening we pulled out a sturdy slab with legs from underneath the bench seat. The legs, attached along the edge, supported the panel of wood and our bodies perfectly. We laid hay-filled mattresses over the wood and only had to change the hay twice a year. Each morning we laid the mattresses over the upper balcony, far enough under the extended roof that inclement weather never caused an issue.

The bedroom, intended for sleeping in the summer, seldom got used. More often than not, on hot summer nights, my sisters and I chose to go out to the barn, spread out fresh soft hay, and then make our beds on blankets. We fell asleep listening to the familiar sounds of the farm. The night's music—crickets chirped their songs, owls hooted while they hunted the woods, and a rabbit screamed when caught. These were exciting and scary sounds to a small boy.

Hot summers eliminated any cooking on the woodstove, so we used our small summer kitchen behind the house. The next building, divided in three parts, served several purposes. In the first section we stored the wood, all the hay, alfalfa, and feed for our animals for the winter. The cool underground cellar proved perfect for the wine vats.

We parked our wagon and stored farm tools in the second section, leaving the furthest section from the home for the animals. Last, but not least, behind the last building was the outhouse. Winter, summer, spring, or fall we had to make the long walk behind the barn.

• • •

In the winter, we all slept in the main room to stay warm. While still young, each night I chose which sister to snuggle against on her portion of the long bench bed. Lucretia, third to the oldest and prettiest, talked to me a lot which made me feel special. I would have chosen her bed every night, but did not want to make my other sisters jealous.

One night, when I was about five years old, Lucretia, who

liked to tease me, asked me what girlfriend I had and who I wanted to marry.

"The lady has not yet had the girl," I answered.

Giggles filled the room from all sides.

• • •

In my eyes, my mother was the most beautiful of all the ladies in the village. Her shiny dark brown hair, worn in a long braid, wound like a crown perched on her head. Her bright eyes reflected the joy of life, and her smile seldom left her face.

She filled our house with laughter and song, and won the appreciation and respect of many of the village women. Our gate became the favorite gathering place, and my mother, the main source of entertainment and gossip.

Of course, those were days of no electricity or indoor plumbing, television, movie theaters, or stores in which to shop. Once they finished work, it did not take long before they came to our home. Our house was the place to engage in neighborhood chatter—laughing and talking about husbands and kids.

I could not walk into the house without being showered with hugs and kisses. My mother enjoyed making my favorite foods and saved me a special portion. However, doting on me did not keep her from teaching me one of my most important obedience lessons. She only punished me once. I never forgot.

A neighbor boy and I had sneaked into a back field close to the neighbor's yard where a mangy dog never stopped barking. We hid in the tall, mature potato plants and lobbed dirt clods over the fence. The dog went into a barking frenzy. We thought it pretty funny, and I admit I enjoyed it—until I got home.

Evidently the potato plants did not hide us. The neighbor lady had promptly gone to where my mother and sisters worked in our front yard to make clothing thread from the hemp plant they cooked, dried, and prepared for spinning. She informed my mother and sisters of my actions.

Later, as I stepped through the gate to go into the house, my mother stopped me.

"Not in this house, anymore."

My heart jumped. I am sure fear showed on my face.

"Who sent you to that house to throw dirt clods at the dog to make it bark and bring shame on us? I don't need this kind of boy."

My mother was always straightforward with me, so I believed I could not live in my house, anymore. I sat on the road by the gate, scared. I cried repeatedly.

What would I do? Where would I go?

After what seemed at least an hour—the longest in my life—she came out. I got up off the ground, stood before her, and tried to wipe away my tears with the backs of my hands.

In a soft voice she said, "You know what, Nelu? If you say you're sorry for what you did, I'll forgive you, now, but if you ever do it again, don't even bother to come into this house."

Joy filled my heart.

"I'm sorry, Mama."

She wrapped her arms around me as I hugged her tightly. Together, we walked into the house.

Relief flooded through me. At age five, with no conceivable options, I had been convinced I would die.

• • •

My father taught me my second life-altering obedience lesson. He had told me to help my sister bring the cows down from the field. Even as a child, I could be persuasive. I talked her into doing it without me.

Father caught me and wanted to know why I had not obeyed. Now, no six-year-old has a legitimate excuse for disobeying, so my father selected a thin branch from a bush and switched me once on the back of my leg. He ordered me to go relieve my sister and finish the job. Though the punishment was not harsh, I never forgot it because I knew I had disappointed my father.

On free days, I asked to go work with him instead of playing with the neighbor kids, but he encouraged me otherwise.

"Son, you'll spend all your days working soon enough. Go play."

I resisted.

"No, Father, I want to go with you."

Often, he gave in. At my father's side, I learned all about horticulture and wine-making. My father had learned the craft after his two years as a World War I (WWI) prisoner of war in Italy when a village farmer offered him work in his vineyard. When he returned to Romania, he met my mother and they married. After a couple years, he planted the vineyard for wine and a source of family income.

Working hard beside my father made one thing clear to me. I did not want to be a farmer.

I learned many of life's lessons while sitting next to Father on the wagon seat. He would point at the houses we passed, and tell me about the people living within. He shared things that happened in their lives based on decisions they had made, good and bad.

He elaborated about how some had squandered blessings or inheritances, and then suffered the consequences. Good decisions or bad choices, in a village that size little remained hidden. Lessons about right and wrong, integrity, and personal responsibility were frequent.

Aside from my father's strong influence, my two favorite cousins, Alexander and John, acted as my mentors. They encouraged me to believe I could do anything I wanted. As long as I did my best, possibilities were endless.

Somehow the idea to be like them or better was planted deep in my mind. I do not know how or why. I just know.

Consumed with the desire to learn, I wanted to go to school when I was seven, but my birthday, one month later than the cut-off date, prevented it. My mother, who was conveniently stubborn and very persuasive, talked the school officials into allowing me to attend without getting credit for it. That meant I attended first grade twice. Happy to be in school, I did not care.

I did not know the importance of that year: 1945. It was the very last year in Romania when the school day began with prayer after we greeted the teacher.

• • •

Our lack of paved roads and other creature comforts proved to be a blessing in disguise; not only for Cergaul Mare, but also for the other small villages throughout Romania.

In 1939, at the beginning of WWII, Romania had remained

neutral. Once France fell and Britain pulled out of continental Europe, the Romanian government—under the leadership of Ion Antonescu—allied with Germany under the pretext of protecting Romania's oil fields. Essentially, the Germans invaded their ally, Romania.

Ion Antonescu and the Iron Guard, in conjunction with the Germans, were responsible for the murder or imprisonment of tens of thousands of Jews, Christians from several denominations, gypsies, and minorities. Many died from brutal torture.

While Romanians in the large urban areas suffered horrifically, life carried on as usual in my village during those years. We were fortunate not to experience the hardships of war. We never saw the evil of the Iron Guard, or the persecutions of the Jews and Christians. For that, I am very grateful.

To those who experienced the horrors of the German occupation, Allied bombings, food shortages, imprisonments, rapes, hunger, and daily fear, news of the war's end brought hope. They truly believed life would get better once the Nazis left. They were wrong—the Russians were coming.

John's oldest sister Marioara and parents Anica and Roman Muntean.

CHAPTER 2

FAITH IN THE SHADOWS

Even though I walk through the valley of the shadow of death,
I fear no evil; for Thou art with me . . .
—Psalm 23:4, NASB

THE SUMMER OF 1946 LIFE changed for everyone—even for that of a soon to be eight-year-old boy. Two opposite philosophies became part of my everyday life: Marxist Socialism was on a march across the nation in an effort to capture the hearts and minds of the citizenry. My heart, however, was captured by a man named Jesus.

As a family, we attended the Roman Catholic Church located in the village where I served as an altar boy and sang the responses in the liturgy. One Sunday afternoon, my older sisters invited our mother to go to the community hall where a group of young people called the Army of God were singing and preaching.

There were about thirty families in our village which belonged to the group. The priest allowed them to use our church most Sunday afternoons, except this one.

Marioara and Lucretia begged, "Mother, please come with us to hear them. They sing so pretty."

Mother agreed to go with them, but when the three walked out the gate past a cluster of chatting ladies, one of them stopped her.

"Anica, where are you going? We want you to stay and talk with us."

"My daughters invited me to go listen to some boys sing and preach from the Bible."

Her friend responded in alarm, "No, you don't want to go there. You might change your religion and become a *pocait*."

To refer to someone as a repentant Pentecostal was a terrible insult—absolutely derogatory. It was equivalent to the *N* word.

Mother smiled and replied, "No. There's nothing in the whole world that could make me change my religion. My daughters asked me and I'm happy to go with them."

However, that afternoon did change the lives of our family forever. Just like the Gentiles in the New Testament upon first hearing of the Messiah, Jesus of Nazareth, Mother believed. Something changed within her which she did not understand.

My mother's joy and passion for Jesus was evident to everyone around her, especially us. At times, the desire to pray overwhelmed her which caused her to drop to her knees. However, she was not prepared for the surge of electricity that spread through her body, so she quit.

This happened for several days, no matter what room she was in. This experience frightened her so much each time, she quit praying. One day, her desire to pray was so strong when she fell to her knees, words she never heard before flowed from out of her mouth.

Combined with the electricity which raced all over her body, it frightened her even more. She did not know what to do because throughout that day, every time she attempted to pray in her native tongue, another language came forth.

This continued for several days until she decided to go see a friend whom she trusted. This lady and her husband, who happened to be our mayor before the Communist takeover, were good friends of my parents. The woman had a good understanding of the Bible.

Mother said, "This is what is happening. I go to say my prayers and another language comes out of my mouth. Then a strange feeling moves all over my skin. It keeps happening, and I don't know what to do. I feel the fire in my heart to pray, but I'm afraid."

Her friend threw up her hands and said, "Praise God, you experienced the baptism of the Holy Spirit, just like it happened in the second chapter of Acts to the followers of Jesus."

Her friend then read the Scriptures which calmed my mother's fears.

For the next two weeks, she went about the house singing and praying in tongues. By then, everyone in the village knew. If someone did not, Mother was happy to tell them.

One Sunday afternoon about three weeks later, Father asked Mother if she wanted to go to the afternoon service. What happened to her was the talk of the town. Even knowing people would be watching her and something could happen, fear did not stop her.

At that time, the men and women sat apart during the Catholic services. When my parents came into the church and separated to their respective areas, my mother knelt prior to going into the pew.

Protocol meant a person went from one statue to another kneeling, praying, and kissing the feet of the statue. Mother simply moved into the pew.

At the end of the service, the leader asked her to pray the benediction. She threw up her hands and opened her mouth to pray. Her prayer came out in tongues. She did not care and was not afraid, so she continued to pray.

Chaos erupted. It was as though lightening divided the church congregation.

Those who knew my mother said, "We know this woman. She's a godly woman and wouldn't make this up."

Others did what they still do today: they said speaking in tongues was for the early church only. Some even attributed it to the devil.

The schism was deep. Half the congregation chose to go forward in this new revelation. The other half stayed with the priest and Catholic Church. Within a year or so, our village priest was arrested and imprisoned, and then replaced with an Orthodox priest chosen by the Romanian Communist Party.

• • •

When God changed my mother, things began to change within our home as well. We had new rules—one of them was no more dancing. This caused so much upset to my sister, Leontina, that in her anger she pulled out chunks of her hair. She was not a happy girl.

Fancy clothes were done away with, plus the women had to cover their hair lest they be filled with pride. The restrictions, of course, were put in place by hearts that genuinely loved God and wanted to please Him.

A few of the rules made no sense to me. Such as keeping men's hair cut short and not allowing women to wear make-up. Still, Mother encouraged us to strive to please God even in the small things.

The Pentecostal movement had first come to Romania in 1922. There were no churches, seminaries, and, certainly, no pastors. No one knew the difference between the Greek and Hebrew. The movement made its way across the nation through the villages before it reached the cities.

I do not know how the people chose the leader of local fellowships in those days. They were genuine believers wanting to please God and live according to what they read and understood from the Bible.

Not too long after the uproar in the Catholic Church, my mother took me into the large winter barn used to house the sheep. We settled on the clean hay where she told me about Jesus.

I remember it as though it was yesterday. Love for Jesus hit my heart—something I'll never forget. I can go back to that place in my mind and experience it all over again. The depth of faith birthed that day carried me through the hard journey ahead and ignited a fire that burns bright to this day.

A thirst to learn the Bible consumed me. By the time I was ten, I had studied almost the entire Bible with the father of a friend of mine. I loved God's Word.

• • •

At first welcomed as liberators, a million Russian soldiers swept into Romania like a swarm of locusts which spreads across the land, stripping it of all vegetation. In the book *In God's Underground*, Richard Wurmbrand, a Romanian Christian minister writes: "The new occupiers had only one idea in life: to drink, rob, and ravage the "capitalist exploiters." Thousands of women of all ages and conditions were raped by soldiers who burst into their homes."[1]

My sister, Lucretia, worked as a tailor's apprentice in the city with other young girls. Her employer protected them by dressing them as elderly women, instructing them how to walk and act feeble—it worked. The soldiers ignored them.

At the end of WWII when King Michael and a group of political leaders met in Moscow to discuss the post-war world, an agreement was struck between Stalin and Churchill. "In fact, its terms were used to strip the country of its entire navy, most of its merchant fleet, half its rolling stock, and every automobile. Farm produce, horses, cattle, and all stocks of oil and petrol were carried off to Russia."[2] They also kidnapped Romanians.

The Germans had murdered three-quarters of a million Jews, but those who avoided capture and imprisonment soon learned they were still marked by the Soviets. Jews as well as Romanians were taken off the streets to go work in the Siberian mines and fields as slave labor.

The Russian soldiers kidnapped men and women alike, many right from their beds in the dead of night. Without even an opportunity to cover themselves, innocent people were shipped like livestock by truck and train to Siberia. Few ever returned.

One of my wife's brothers-in-law, however, escaped. For

months, he lived off the land, and slept by day and walked by night. He gradually made his way back to Romania and his family. As he traveled, he saw workers toiling naked in the fields of Odesa.

In spite of all the promises of the new Socialist leadership, within a short time Romania became a starving nation, especially in larger cities.

Before this, 80 percent of Romanian productivity came from agriculture. The citizens in small towns and villages owned their land, worked their fields, and tended their crops and herds. They were totally self-sufficient, except when they needed hardware or food items they could not produce.

The larger farms employed day laborers. The towns and cities were filled with shops, privately-owned by people who had learned trades, developed skills, and worked hard to earn what they had.

We call them the middle-class. The Communists called them the enemy—capitalists, entrepreneurs, individuals, the bourgeoisie, and the *haves*.

In Bucharest, the capital of Romania, the Little Paris of Eastern Europe, Marxists did everything to eliminate all opposition to their leadership and agenda. When they had come to power on March 5, 1945, the Romanian Communist Party (RCP), a pro-Soviet government used the country's political structure, educational system, and trade unions to make Romania completely subservient to the Soviet Union.

Over the next two years, they dissolved the major democratic parties, with the forced abdication of King Michael in December 1947. Until 1945, only a few thousand Romanians had belonged to the Communist Party. Within a short time the numbers grew to millions. Having the party card often made the difference between going hungry and having food to eat.

Within six months of the Communist takeover, the effects poured in like a raging river. First into the regions; then the counties; next, the smaller cities; and, at last, the villages—even those smaller than ours. Within the first full year, our small village boasted a government presence.

Like an octopus with thousands of tentacles, the RCP attached itself to every part of Romanian home life. The home, workplace, schools, and churches—nothing and no one escaped them.

They arrived in our village with smiles on their faces and told us of all the wonderful things they were going to do for us. They filled the ears of the men with empty promises of six hour workdays, great wages, and three suits of clothes with all the accessories. For some, the lure was too much to resist.

My father, wise enough to know the Communist Party spoke lies, met with men in our home. He warned them not to put their faith in the Marxist promises.

• • •

My second year of school, which consisted of repeating the first grade, was very different from the previous one. Instead of a respectful greeting of "good morning" or "good day" to our teacher, and reciting the Lord's Prayer, we stood and saluted our teacher.

"Long Live the Republic," we sang a short chorus with those words. We were instructed to address our elders on the street the same way. The adults simply turned their heads away—some hid a snicker, some their anger.

If caught not giving a proper response, the adult could have been brought in by the Securitate to give an explanation. No one wanted to be questioned by the secret police.

Although it took some years to implement other policies of change, the restructure of the educational system was immediate. Lenin fully believed if he could indoctrinate a student for four years, the socialist ideology would remain with the child throughout life.

The Stalinist Soviets evidently agreed. Students were required to learn Russian and wear uniforms. We were called Stalin's Young Pioneers.

The indoctrination of Communist ideology began in earnest. Beginning in the fifth grade, we students were required to wear uniforms, with little red scarves around our necks which we were supposed to kiss before putting on. I never did.

We were required to attend every meeting of any high ranking Communist official regardless of where it was held. Uniforms had to be clean and pressed. We either sat or stood without moving.

We were required to clap and cheer on queue. The speeches would be filled with all the reasons socialism was so wonderful and how the students were the future leadership. The patriotic music and enthusiastic speech seemed almost hypnotic.

We students were the future leadership of the RCP. Therefore, the teachers or professors who did not align with the new party policies disappeared. We were told they transferred to other schools. Not true.

I became a target at school. I began to pay the price for my faith, just as my parents were. Persecution of Christian students became the norm. We were ridiculed in front of our classmates and called pocait, fanatic, uneducated, and worse.

Humiliation and punishment were daily experiences in some classes. I learned right away to remain silent when they would try to degrade me for being a pocait.

Not only in our school, but across the entire school system, Christian students were called to the front of the room. The comments were pretty typical: "This is a pocait. They don't deserve to live or be among us. The government does so much for them—provides them with everything and educates them, but they're retarded and an embarrassment to the country."

Often, when a Christian student performed poorly the professor asked, "What kind of God lets you fail?"

On the other hand when we excelled, they said, "This student is very intelligent. An intelligence accumulated through the efforts of the RCP, but his family believes it comes from God. They believe it comes from the Bible and going to church, but that's foolish. It's stupid."

One of the common forms of punishment for a student included kneeling in the corner on sharp kernels of corn, or pieces of broken nut shells, with the student's hands held high over his or her head. A student being whacked on the head with a ruler, or pulled by an earlobe happened frequently.

Another extremely painful punishment required the tips of a student's fingers brought together, and held upright so the end of the fingers were easily whacked with a stick or ruler. Not once, but many times. By the time it was over the student could not feel the tips of their fingers, or hold a pencil, let alone write.

Almost all students experienced the same or similar punishments at some point. However, Christian students suffered these kinds of punishments simply because they were believers.

I must say whether or not a student suffered severely in this manner depended on how determined the teacher or professor was to rise in the ranks of the Communist Party. Educators who simply wanted to put bread on the table were far less abusive.

Although I experienced some of this treatment, my grades were above average. I learned quickly to keep my mouth shut to avoid harsher treatment.

CHAPTER 3

PLANS

For I know the plans I have for you, declares the Lord, plans
for welfare and not for calamity, to give you a future and a hope.
—Jeremiah 29:11, NASB

IN THE NOT-SO-DISTANT PAST, THE men who had gathered at our home to speak with Father talked of daily happenings. Once the Communists took over, one topic dominated: what was happening in the country.

As a young boy, it impressed me how the men of the neighborhood respected and listened to my father. I stayed out of the way, as quiet as possible, so I could listen to all the conversation. I wanted to learn.

In time, things began to change in the village. A division in mindset developed. About 25 percent of the men in the village were swayed and supported the Socialist agenda. They genuinely believed the promises made by the pro-Soviets. Where there had been trust among neighbors, mistrust developed.

Some of the men in the village who spoke out against the new Communist leadership disappeared in the middle of the night. I thank God my father was not among them. Many never returned, and some only came home after many years in prison. We learned quickly not to denounce the government.

Romanian people never knew who was genuinely safe to talk to because informing on neighbors became a way of life. It was not unusual for someone to turn on friends, and even family members. Within a year, the women no longer gathered at our gate to gossip and talk about their families.

Our beautiful, vibrant, productive country no longer existed. Fear stalked the streets, and bellies groaned from hunger. Families were torn apart, as fathers or mothers disappeared for months, years, sometimes forever.

• • •

Indoctrination of the adult population was never attempted. Instead, promises which never materialized were made in an attempt to win the hearts and minds of the populace. Failing that, laws were established. People either followed them or paid the price; it was that simple.

The first efforts to influence the Romanian leadership—in cities, towns, or villages—to come alongside and join the new government failed. The great minds—scholars, teachers, government leaders, and business owners who spoke against or resisted the Communist policies and agenda—were the first to go. Beatings and torture were commonplace as a result of such defiance.

Communist officials resorted to finding the uneducated—mostly day laborers, union members, and gypsies—to fill positions of leadership in the cities, towns, and villages. These were people who followed without question, and wanted to believe and trust in the government. They fell for the empty promises.

• • •

Just one half mile from our village a farmer owned a large portion of land. Every year he tilled the ground, and planted many rows of corn. Then, he sectioned off the fields in equal portions, and offered each worker in our village a portion.

It was their responsibility to weed the rows and pick the corn. Once the harvest monies were paid, the landowner always split the profits 50 percent. It was a fair system that worked extremely well.

Communists arrested the farmer, confiscated his property, and put him in prison. A gypsy was put in charge of the large farm. No legitimate reason was offered for the farmer's imprisonment. The workers were told they owned the whole land, it was theirs.

Communist officials promised shorter work days and a share in the profits. None of their promises materialized. Those who were naïve worked and harvested the crop, and stood shocked when the government said, "Sorry boys, there isn't any left for you."

Between the broken promises and the ignorance of the new manager, the farm was destroyed within two years. The fields lay fallow.

My father asked the gypsy, "How can you run this farm without having any experience, and unable to read or write?"

He replied, "They told me I could run it out of my head."

Another man was installed as the new mayor to our small

village. He only had a fourth grade education. No one in the village wanted the position under the Communists.

• • •

Within the first few years of Soviet-controlled Romania, religious persecution was responsible for the murder and imprisonment of tens of thousands of spiritual leaders who refused to bow. The only legal religion was the Orthodox Church—which was, at that time, the largest denomination in Romania.

The Soviet government paid the salaries of priests and bishops who toed the party line. Clergy were rewarded for informing on parishioners after confessional visits. It was not uncommon for the parishioner to be arrested and imprisoned.

Churches such as Baptist, Pentecostal, Lutheran, Seventh-day Adventist, and Evangelical Orthodox, which was part of The Army of the Lord, were considered sects and put under the Communist-controlled Ministry of Cults, which had paid informers in every church body across Romania who attended every service, wedding, and baptism.

If a pastor said anything considered anti-government propaganda, or appeared to have anti-social activity, the informant reported it. The pastor was then taken by the Securitate to be interrogated. Thousands of pastors were imprisoned. Lies were worth just as much money, and were often used in order to get paid.

Christians were considered the enemy of Marxist doctrine. Even today, Socialists around the globe want to eliminate Christianity—they call it the opiate of the people. It promotes the individual, the value of a human being, God's love for His creation, and, of course, belief in an afterlife. A man or woman of strong faith in Christ is not easily persuaded or broken in spirit.

Known Christian leaders were constantly watched for any possible violation. The church eventually went underground.

A major teaching of the Marxist Communist doctrine is there is no God, so man is nothing, but matter, to live, work for the party, die, and return to nothing more than a pile of dust. Everything is done for the party and furtherance of its ideology and power.

Fourteen million Romanians attended the Orthodox Church, while 2.5 million were either Roman or Greek Catholic. The Communist government forced the Catholics to join the Orthodox Church. Those who resisted unification paid a heavy price, whether or not they were clergy. Orthodox priests aligned with the Communists, and were put in places of leadership within the church and throughout the country—the government paid them well.

Across Romania, church schools, private high schools, seminaries, monasteries, and convents were closed, and most of the priests and nuns were imprisoned. Literally, all hell had broken loose. Christians suffered much greater torture for their faith. They experienced intense beatings and faced starvation.

Richard and Sabina Wurmbrand, pastors in Romania, tell the martyrs' story in three books, *In God's Underground*, *The Pastor's Wife*, and *Tortured for Christ*. Richard and Sabina were, in fact, imprisoned—Sabina was jailed for three years while Richard was incarcerated twice for a combination of fourteen and a half years. Their books tell of the unbelievable brutality prisoners suffered.

One punishment Richard Wurmbrand was well-acquainted with was the Carcer, a favorite form of torture by the prison authority. Wurmbrand writes: "I was taken down the corridor to a cupboard built into a wall, just high enough to stand in and twenty inches square, with a few air holes and one for food to be pushed through. The guard thrust me in and closed the door. Sharp points stung my back. I jerked forward, to be pierced again in the chest."[3] Blindfolded, the prisoner immediately learned not to move. Sharp projectiles pierced from all sides. Only by standing still was impalement avoided. Some prisoners stood inside for days.

In his book *Tortured for Christ,* Wurmbrand shares "Christians were also placed in ice-box "refrigerator cells" which were so cold that frost and ice covered the inside. I was thrown into one while I had very little clothing on. Prison doctors would watch through an opening until they saw symptoms of freezing to death then they would give a signal and guards would rush in to take us out..."[4] The guards also took particular delight in forcing Christians to drink urine and eat human feces, a perverted caricature of communion.

When Richard Wurmbrand testified before the Internal Security Subcommittee of the U.S. Senate he told of unbelievable, but true, torture such as "Christians tied to crosses for four days and nights. The crosses were placed on the floor and hundreds of prisoners had to fulfill their bodily necessities over the faces and bodies of the crucified ones."[5]

Wurmbrand's books tell not only of great suffering, but also of amazing victory in Christ. Where evil abounds, Christ reveals His love even more.

Those of us on the outside heard these stories. No one was safe, not even the top Communist leadership.

In his book, *In God's Underground*, Wurmbrand tells of his arrest in 1948, and being the first prisoner in Calea Rahova, the new prison. His first cellmate was Comrade Lucretiu Patrascanu, the Communist leader, who was only there for one week. His crime? He came from a family of landowners, so he was viewed as a western communist—more Romanian than Red. Thus, he was considered a threat to the Soviet agenda for Romania.

Wurmbrand recounts: "The second prisoner in my brand-new cell was the man who brought communism to power in our country."[6] I share this information to show not even party leaders were safe, regardless of rank or position in the hierarchy. Anyone—everyone—was expendable for the greater cause or another party member's power grab.

The picture Marxist Socialism likes to present to the world is quite different than the reality we experienced. In Romania, it was about taking control of everything—and take control, they did.

On June 11, 1948, the Communist government put in place Decree 119 which nationalized all private companies and their assets. Likewise in April 1950, Decree 92 instituted the confiscation of a huge number of private homes and land—private property ownership is considered evil and a threat to the communist ideology. By the following spring all land was removed from private ownership without compensation.

The lips of the people began to whisper hope for a new savior: America. They believed the Americans were coming, but they never did.

• • •

For the seven years I was in school, my grades were excellent in the mathematic sciences, and my dream to become an engineer burned strong in my heart. I wanted to build bridges and roads.

Academically, I was at the top of my class, which was beneficial. When I reached the sixth grade, it was common for the professor to send students to me to assist them with homework assignments.

In Romania, the primary grades ran from first to seventh grade. I was fourteen years old when I graduated. Unfortunately, our village had no opportunities for higher education, which was not a problem for me since I had my heart set on the school in Sibiu.

The high schools in Romania specialized in teaching trades. As always, the total students who tested far outnumbered the slots available. The top pupils earned scholarships while others paid for their education. Students who were accepted, but did not reside locally, had to live in the dormitories.

The graduates from the school in Sibiu became the engineers who designed and built the bridges and roads. The school's base subjects were math, algebra, and geometry—the subjects in which I excelled. This school was my best option if my dream were to come true.

My father walked in a straight line over the hills to register me for the entrance exams. Whereas Sibiu was one hundred miles round trip by car, across the high hills it was approximately thirty miles round trip.

When it came time for me to leave, my parents sent me off on the train prepared to stay the ten days required for testing. There were only forty openings for the class; however, five hundred applicants took the exams. I felt quite confident I was going to pass, as these subjects came relatively easy to me.

When I finally finished my exam, I noticed the two boys directly in front of me. Their table abutted mine. They had made a number of mistakes. When they came back to the dorm room, I told them what I had observed.

A man, who turned out to be the father of one boy and uncle to the other, was very disturbed to hear about these mistakes. He suddenly announced he needed to go back home to Oltenia, in the southwest part of Romania. He said he would return, but he did not explain why he had decided to leave.

Two weeks later, when I returned to the school just prior to its opening for classes, I looked at the test scores. Frankly, I was quite confident I had scored high and earned a spot. Out of the five hundred students who had tested, one hundred and fifty passed.

I searched for my name; it was number forty-one. Again, there were only forty openings for the class. I had missed by only one spot. I stared at the scores and tried to make sense of the results when a man approached me. He was the school security guard.

"How's it going young man? Did you make it or not?"

"If there was one more spot, it would be mine. I'm number forty-one."

He studied me for a moment and said, "You didn't come here from home, did you? If you had come from home, you wouldn't have placed number forty-one, but number one."

I had no idea what he meant.

"But I did come from home."

"I'm sure you didn't come from home, but then maybe you don't know what that means."

At that he walked away.

He was right. I did not know what he was talking about. I turned back to the list. Both of those other boys were in the top forty. They had been accepted, mistakes and all. As I thought about it I began to get an idea what the security guard meant. I remembered the father of one of those boys had left to go home. When he returned he came with money and gifts for the professors.

Very distressed, I went to the school office where I received all of the exam documents. I was told with my exam scores I was able to attend any advanced school in the country without re-testing.

If my scores were so high, then why couldn't I go to this school?

They told me the other options were to wait and test at this school again the following year, or hope another student dropped out or withdrew. My dream to earn an engineering degree could only be realized by attending this school.

I returned home very upset.

• • •

The following year when I returned to register for the exams, I was told to go back home and convince my father to give up his farm to the collective. Furthermore, I was told if I was not able to come back with supporting documentation, I should not bother to come back at all.

That was why I was number forty-one on the list.

It became clear that if I had "come from home" with signed documentation releasing my parents land to the collective, my name would have been number one. How the guard knew about my possible placement, I do not know.

The ideology of the collective abolishes the privilege of private property ownership. The government owns and controls any and all farmland, production, and distribution.

My parents worked their whole life to have a business-farm, and there was no way I would have ever asked them to give it up. I kept the knowledge to myself.

They were heartbroken for me and knew my dream. So, they contacted my cousins—one was a judge and the other, the mayor of Blaj. Neither could help. My parents attempted everything they knew to make it happen, and begged God to make it possible.

One night as my mother lay in bed beseeching God on my behalf, she had a vision. She saw herself standing at the wood-stove used for cooking. The stove had one large cooking hole, but three covers of varying size which fit within each other—larger to smaller—thus, varying the size of the opening.

The smallest cover was off the hole and flames were seen. She held a jar of honey in her hand which she tried to force through the smallest opening. No matter how much she pushed to make it fit, it would not. At that point, she looked at the hole and realized if she did not stop, the jar would break and the honey would be destroyed.

What am I doing? She thought.

Then the voice of the Lord spoke to her.

"This is the way you are trying to put your boy in the fire."

Immediately, she understood God had told them to stop their efforts to get me into the school. The next morning, her eyes filled with tears as she shared the vision with me. My parents wanted so much to help me, but she understood God gave her the vision as a warning.

I was not happy about them stopping their efforts, but accepted what she said. Deep inside, I recognized it as God's direction, but I was disappointed. I had hoped being able to design, and build bridges and roads was to be my road to success.

Eventually, I would understand God had protected me.

CHAPTER 4

THE GROANING

When the righteous increase, the people rejoice, but when a
wicked man rules, the people groan.
—Proverbs 29:2, NASB

FIFTEEN YEARS OLD, AND MY formal education was over. I was
angry at God.

How could I feel that way?

I knew what my mother told me was true, but it is not always
easy for a boy to give up on a dream. I loved God and my parents,
so I turned my anger toward communism; a true hatred began to
take root in my heart. I wanted no part of the Socialist system, yet
it forced me to live within its structure.

• • •

No matter how large or small a community, none had escaped the Communist policies, or the devastation they brought
to Romania. Christian persecution continued to sweep across the
country as believers were arrested in their homes, churches, and
sometimes kidnapped off the street to never be heard from again.

My current pastor and friend, Pastor Lazar Gog, tells of what his father, Victor, went through on Easter Sunday, 1955. A lay minister in the small village of Galpia, he was preaching to a small number of people in a church when the doors burst open. Three people walked in: the village's Municipal Secretary of the Communist Party, a police officer, and an Orthodox priest. They arrested the adults in the church for attending an anti-social activity meeting.

Young and old, they forced them to march fifty-five miles to the city of Cluj. They were allowed no food, little water, and no stopping. The local police squads changed from village to village, but there was no rest for the people. The march took two and a half days.

When they arrived in Cluj, they were taken to the courthouse and put in the dungeon below. All forty-two were put on trial and found guilty, and then sentenced to three months and one day in prison. All were given probation, except Pastor Gog's father and six other men, who were considered the leaders. His mother, Maria, along with the others had to find transportation home.

It turned out the extra day allowed the prison officials to determine how long a prisoner was incarcerated. In the case of Pastor Gog's father and the other men, it pleased the prison officials to keep them an additional four and a half months.

The men were kept for seven and a half months of forced labor. They experienced beatings, torture, and starvation. They were pressured to become informers. During that time, without having been fed, they were taken to different villages to do forced labor. Local Pentecostal believers risked their lives by bribing the village guards to slip the men food.

Many years later, after Pastor Gog was a newly ordained Pentecostal pastor, the secret police knocked on his apartment door in the middle of the night. He lost count, but he said it happened fifteen to twenty times in a three-month period. They took him into the forest, made him lie on the ground, and then begin psychological torture in an effort to get him to become an informer against his congregation. Their threats to kill and make him fish bait fell on deaf ears.

· · ·

Over the entire forty-four years of Communist rule, Christians suffered horrific persecution. Sometimes, I wonder if anyone ever stops to ask why.

Why do the Socialists really consider Christianity such a threat?

The control of the church was total. The early whispers of religious persecution in the late '40s became screams by my fifteenth year of age. Yes, the Orthodox Church was sanctioned, but it was led by those loyal to the Marxist doctrine. The other denominations, controlled by the Ministry of Cults, were permitted to hold services, but they were classified as sects, and micro-managed by the party.

In some cases, the party even controlled how many parishioners attended a church service, which was the case regarding Richard Wurmbrand once he was released from prison. The government had given him a small church in Orsova.

Richard reports: "The Communist Department of Cults told me it had thirty-five members in it and warned that it must never have thirty-six. I was told that I must be their agent and report to the secret police on every member and keep all youth away. This is how the Communists use churches as their "tool" of control."[7]

The party dictated how many services were allowed per week. Baptisms or christenings had to be applied for, and anyone in attendance needed to be listed. Pastors had to report every other Monday to the regional inspector of cults for interrogation to confirm his report about how many congregants attended each service—and the subject of his sermon—matched the informer's report. His report had better match the informer's because any variance endangered the pastor.

It was a practice in our church to honor older members. Often, they were invited to lead the congregation in prayer. One Sunday, just after the last worship song was sung, an older member led the congregation in prayer. He then announced one of the brothers in Christ who sat in the congregation was to preach the message. The man he indicated remained seated, so the brother repeated the announcement, and invited the man to come to the pulpit to preach the Gospel.

Instead of coming forward, the man stood, and then bolted out of the church. He was an informer. They were everywhere.

Believers had no other recourse other than to go underground. Any non-sanctioned prayer meetings, church services, or gatherings were considered illegal. To smuggle Bibles and Christian materials into Romania was very dangerous. If believers were caught—prison awaited them.

However, the underground church began to flourish while thousands languished in prison for their faith. News of the church's persecution soon reached the free-world and questions were raised—not only from the human rights advocacy groups, but also church leaders from the West wanted answers. Romania's leadership reassured them there was religious freedom in Romania, but, of course, it was a lie.

When church leaders, dignitaries, or foreign diplomats from other countries visited to investigate, they were welcomed into church services—filled to capacity. The Orthodox priest delivered the sermon and people sang. Yet, in reality, the church was filled with RCP members and their families. This charade happened often, as well-compensated Romanian church leaders reassured their western counterparts. It was easy to understand why these acts of deception were believed.

The Communist leaders were very clever in their deceit. The Western world delegates appeared to fall for it. I often wondered whether or not their acceptance was due to a belief they could not prove otherwise, or if they were truly fooled. Regardless, they went about proclaiming the religious freedom within Romania.

Within Romanian borders, however, Christians understood to speak openly about anything spiritual at work or in the marketplace put them in danger. Relentless persecution of the church and individual Christians prevailed throughout the land.

• • •

From the very beginning of their takeover of government in 1945, the Romanian Communist Party moved quickly to implement Stalinist Communism. One of the first moves was to disarm people. Citizens were given fifteen days to surrender all their guns to the police.

No firearms were allowed in anyone's possession, not even for hunting. Except, of course, for the paid hunter whose job it was to make certain no Romanian citizen driven by hunger killed an animal to eat. The paid hunter did not hunt animals, he hunted humans.

For citizens, failure to comply meant an automatic fifteen years in prison. There were those who resisted, of course. However, they paid the price when the police broke into their homes in the dead of night to search for suspected firearms.

My father had no firearms, so we were not in any danger at that time.

Dictators such as Stalin, Hitler, and Mao knew the only way to secure power was to completely disarm citizens. Depending on whose research is used, there are estimates of 110–259 million killed by their governments during the 1900s. Facts unequivocally prove unarmed citizens cannot defend themselves against a totalitarian government bent on total control.

Deep fear of the Securitate ruled the populace. The secret police struck terror into the hearts and minds of the citizens. Thus, they were able to move quickly against all opposition.

Lieutenant General Ion Mihai Pacepa's book, *Red Horizons*, relates another ugly face of the Romanian Communist Party with a practice that began once the state of Israel was recognized by the United Nations. Romania ransomed Jews to Israel.

In late 1949, it cost fifty to one hundred American dollars to buy a Jewish man's or woman's freedom. Pastor Richard Wurmbrand, considered a hero to the Romanian people and a thorn in the flesh of the Communists "was released in a general amnesty in 1964, and again continued his underground ministry. Realizing the great danger of a third imprisonment, Christians in Norway negotiated with the Communist authorities for his release from Romania. The Communist government had begun "selling" their political prisoners. The "going price" for a prisoner was $1,900; the price for Wurmbrand was $10,000."[8]

Obviously, in the fifteen years of trading Jews for money the Communist government had learned their value.

• • •

Our village, Cergaul Mare, was considered small. Although we had been visited by Communist officials, the total turn-over or collectivization of our farms took longer than other more populated areas of Romania. Collectivism in Romania under communism destroyed our country which was once known for its amazing agricultural productivity. The ideology may have been appealing to some, but its implementation never worked.

Private property ownership does not work in this system. Remember this: under communism, an individual exists for the benefit of the Socialist agenda. A human being is considered dust. He or she lives, serves the party, and dies—period.

• • •

Most Americans do not know the first couple of years at Plymouth, Massachusetts, under the leadership of Governor William Bradford, Puritans tried collectivism. Christians who wanted no part of the old world greed, corruption, and materialism adopted Plato's brand of communism. Governor Bradford's diary tells how the less energetic workers failed to do their fair share which angered the more industrious workers. The end result after two years was a harvest so poor the majority of colonists starved to death.

The next year Governor Bradford divided the plots of land, based on family size, for the survivors to farm as they wished and keep what they produced. That year's harvest was not only enough for the family's needs, but there was also enough left to trade for other needs. They learned ownership creates incentive.

Lenin and Stalin, however, took their form of collectivism to the extreme. After the two world wars, countries occupied by Soviets—forced into collectivism—suffered close to thirty million deaths from starvation.

In the Ukraine alone the Kulaks, peasant farmers, were systemically starved to death because they did not bow to Stalin taking their land for the collective. The farmers killed their livestock, and burned their crops to keep everything out of the hands of the Soviets. In the end, many were driven to cannibalism. Ten million people, including three million children, died.

Thank God, in Romania, landowners were not so brutally forced to release their properties to the collective. The Communist leadership in Romania took a softer line. Still not all Romanians accepted the takeover quietly.

Most resisted as long as possible—my father being one of them. Taxes were increasingly levied, and production quotas were raised until the owners *willingly* gave up their land. Of course, in many cases threats and beatings were used to speed up the process.

The proletariat day laborers' and union workers' minds had been filled with many empty promises. This new system, supposedly the answer to the proletariat's prayer, turned into a nightmare for all, but those who joined the Communist Party. Of course, the Communists with their party cards had special warehouses filled with all kinds of foods, produce, meats, eggs, and more. However, the rest of the working class stood in food lines only to be turned away continually: the shelves were empty.

• • •

Not being able to continue my education, I started to learn the tailoring trade. Two of my older sisters, Marioara and Lucretia, had finished their tailoring apprenticeships in a nearby city, and had returned home. Our father purchased each of them excellent sewing machines, so they were able to teach me.

Within two years I was very good at it. While it was not my choice profession, it was far better than working in the collectivized farm system.

I lived as normal a life as possible under Communist rule. My faith carried me through the temptations of youth. Shortly after I had committed my life to Jesus, at age seven, I began reading the Bible daily. A friend's father helped me understand biblical truths.

By the age of fifteen, I was joined by a couple friends who loved Jesus as much as me. We often read Scripture together and prayed. We began to ask God to baptize us with the Holy Spirit. One day, I had a feeling.

I told them, "Tonight we'll receive."

I do not know how I knew other than through the Holy Spirit. We met each other in the barn and knelt. Before we even prayed, it happened. The Holy Spirit came upon us, baptizing the three of us—we all began to pray in other tongues.

The leaders in our church were very concerned. At the time, it was their belief the Holy Spirit might be lost if one sinned—no one had any theological training. Since they wanted to exercise their faith carefully in our church, no one was ever baptized before eighteen. They simply did not know what to do with youth our age. Finally, cooler heads prevailed and said if the Holy Spirit chose to baptize us, it must be appropriate.

This experience, and my ongoing walk with the Lord, helped keep me strong in many ways, especially morally where young ladies were concerned. I had a lot of girlfriends; however, my parents and sisters had instructed me often about proper behavior around girls.

Of course, my sisters insisted I treat all girls like ladies. Their instruction, and the very real fear of going to hell, helped curb certain urges.

• • •

In Romania, the law required all young men to report for military duty the year of their twentieth birthday. So, I—along with the other young men from my village—received notice to report for the normal physicals.

They processed us, performed the health exams, recorded all the information, and then sent us home to be called when needed. For some reason, I was separated from the other young men and taken into the captain's office.

The captain was a little taller than me. He welcomed me, and then invited me to sit opposite him at a table which served as his desk. He stared at me for a long a moment, possibly trying to size me up or intimidate me.

I'm not sure.

He began to tell me they knew how much I had wanted additional education. They were also aware of my dream to be an engineer and build bridges and roads. He assured me it could still happen. He rambled about the great future I had ahead of me, and reminded me they were the ones who could make it possible. Up to that point, he almost seemed compassionate.

I wondered how they knew so much. Those dreams had been laid to rest years ago.

He continued to speak as he reached into a drawer and pulled out a piece of paper. He slid it across the table.

"A simple signature on this declaration is all that's needed. In order to keep things simple we drew it up for you. It's the only thing between you and your future."

He pointed to the signature line and then said, "Here. Sign here."

I leaned back and looked at him.

"I would like to read this declaration before signing it, since I didn't write it."

He waited.

It read:

> The undersigned, Ioan Muntean, born October 29, 1938, in Cergaul Mare, Nr.63, declares the following:
>
> I pledge to respect the laws of the Republic Socialist Romania. I will uphold my obligation to my motherland

according to the directive or instructions given by the governing Communist Party and its leader, Comrade Ghorghe Giorghiu Dej. I pledge to deny my faith in God and denounce religious practices.

With everything I had seen, and all the believers had suffered, their audacity and shamelessness still dumbfounded me. I do not know what the officer saw in my expression, but he launched into another effort to reassure me it was only a formality.

"We're not interested in your beliefs; we simply want to have this declaration in your file, and then you'll have every opportunity you hoped for."

My gaze met him square in the eyes.

"If I deny my religious convictions, and this is just a formality, then this is just a lie. How could you trust I'll do what you want me to do?"

He glared at me, and then eyed the gun on his desk.

"Are you going to touch the gun?"

That made no sense to me—then or now—unless he was testing my religious beliefs. There were some faiths, such as Jehovah's Witnesses, which prohibited even the touching of firearms.

I looked at the gun and reached for it. He jumped as if stung by a bee. I still laugh when I remember his reaction.

"No, no, no!" he shouted.

It may have been loaded. I do not know, but I drew back my hand and studied him. Again, the captain pushed the argument for me to sign the declaration, and stressed the benefit to my future. He tried to convince me no one would know.

I replied, "Captain, how can I renounce my strongest conviction, my certainty? God, for me, is a reality and I'd never forsake my faith in Him."

The volume in his voice increased as he, once again, went through a whole list of reasons.

Finally, I said, "Captain, if you give me the whole world, I'll still not sign."

In a moment he was out of his chair, around the end of the table, twelve inches from my face, screaming. He was out of control as he yelled and cursed at me like a drill sergeant screams at his recruits. The difference here is he had the authority to threaten my life—which was exactly what he did. His most chilling threat made was to send me to the Danube River-Black Sea prison camp with criminals.

Shocked, I could not understand why he threatened me so.

John Muntean, age 25.

CHAPTER 5

DELIVERANCE

Deliver me from my enemies, O my God . . .
—Psalm 59:1–3, NASB

I STRAIGHTENED UP IN THE hard office chair with the captain's threat hanging over me. Still, I would not sign.

The Danube River-Black Sea project area was a place where criminals were sent to work the sugarcane fields—often in chest-high water. Many never returned.

Back in 1953, politics put an end to the construction of a canal connecting the Black Sea with the Danube River. However, the concentration camp was never closed. Over two hundred thousand prisoners worked on that project—thousands died.

More than likely, I would dig ditches alongside those who had refused to cooperate with the Socialist system. Others who had resisted giving up their land, or who dared to speak out against the Communist policies and leadership, found themselves sentenced to the Danube Canal project—young and old, men and women, Christians, priests, nuns, landowners, and perceived dissidents. Evidently, my refusal to renounce my faith was reason enough to send me.

Those who found themselves transported to the prison camp were forced to work in life-threatening conditions—the freezing winter, sweltering summer heat, lack of food, and forced labor from dawn until dark were the minor struggles. The camp was a place of death and despair with regular beatings by guards who took delight in torture.

• • •

Though I had not met her yet, my future wife and her family experienced the pain of a family member being imprisoned at the Danube Canal Project. Her eighteen-year-old brother tried to escape to Yugoslavia and failed. When he was caught, he spent two years in this hell hole. She and her parents did not know he had survived until his release when he walked through the front door of their home into their midst. Great rejoicing followed with thanksgiving to the Lord.

• • •

The captain made it clear this was the destiny which awaited me. No matter the threat, I refused to deny my faith. I rejoined the other young men from our village, and returned home to await the military to call me for active duty.

The peril which hung over my head that year was only part of the nightmare I experienced. I almost died and my father did, in fact, die.

Up to 1959, my father and mother did everything possible to meet the government's mandates to avoid collectivization. They were taxed on the property, and then given quotas to meet based on the produce of our livestock and land. At that time, we still had pigs, sheep, chickens, and buffalo. The horses and cows had been taken years before.

Bit-by-bit under this heavy taxation, my parents and the other villagers were forced to sell off their livestock and farm equipment. Finally, with nothing left, but the land and no way to meet the taxes, owners begrudgingly released their land to the collective. All that remained were their homes which sat on a small plot of Earth.

Prior to 1945, before the communist takeover, productive fields and farmyards with horses, cows, sheep, chickens, geese, and pigs existed. By 1959, there was nothing left, except buffalo and some chickens. The buffalo were the only livestock the government wanted no part of. They had been domesticated and trained to work in the fields, pulling the plows and farm equipment, but they refused to perform for strangers.

My mother and I had persuaded my father a few years earlier to buy a couple baby buffalo. My mother and sister talked to them in the barn as if they were having a conversation with little children. Between my mother, sister, and me we trained the buffalo to be very obedient.

The animals were very affectionate and followed me all over the property. After a long day of grazing in the fields, they came to the front of the house to search for me, and grunted several times in an effort to draw me out.

• • •

If I came out onto the porch, they licked my hand, and then turned to enter their stalls in the barn. If I was not there, they came up three of the four steps to the porch and continued to call. When they failed to find me, they covered the entire property, grunting all the way.

Their routine was predictable as they checked around the summer kitchen, and then went into the big sheep barn. If they gave up, they finally went into their stalls in the barn to wait for me.

I enjoyed singing to them, especially as I milked them. If I forgot to sing, they refused to let down their milk, and swung their heads around to eye me, and grunted a reminder.

• • •

Up until the time we lost our land, we had raised wheat and corn. Normally, it was harvested and stored to provide food for the upcoming year. A sudden increase in quota left us with no wheat for flour, so I walked to the flour mill about six miles away to buy a year's supply.

The harvested wheat came in large 120-pound bags. It had to go through the milling process before it became refined enough for bread. I bought eight bags at the mill for our family, and my sister paid for eight bags for her family.

It was my responsibility to help the granary employee process our sixteen bags. I arrived early in the morning and worked all day until about 8:00 PM that night. I hoisted and carried the bags up and down a couple of flights of stairs for each process until the job was completed. Harvesting and threshing the wheat was just the beginning—from kernel to milled baking flour is a multi-faceted process.

At the end of twelve hours, I was exhausted and overheated. My plan was to bring the wagon, pulled by the buffalo, to pick up the sacks of flour the next day. On my walk back home through the forest I reached the top of a hill where a cool breeze blew. It felt nice, so I took off my coat and kept it off until I arrived home.

My mother came to wake me to go to the mill the next morning, but she could not rouse me initially. Slow to wake up, I could not move. I had severe pain all over my body, was paralyzed, and burned with fever.

My mother and father massaged my arms and legs to help me finally stand. They called the doctor assigned to our village. Though it was illegal for doctors to require money of a patient under socialized healthcare, all the doctors did. After my mother paid his fee, he told my parents there was no hope. They should prepare for my burial.

I never knew the cause of my sudden illness, but years later in the United States, I learned it was due to some kind of extreme bacteria. It damaged some valves in my heart which has in recent years created a serious health issue. I thank God it was not a problem until I became older.

For two months my parents tried everything. The prescribed medication did not help, and neither did the medicinal herbs the neighbors brought. I was bedbound, only able to get up to take care of my needs. The pain in my body started at the bottom of my feet, and shot up into the back of my head.

Was I afraid I would die? No.

I did not want to die. I wanted to live. Yet, I suffered such severe pain that if God wanted to take me, I was okay with it.

In desperation my mother went to our neighbor, the oldest man in the village, and talked to him about my illness. He suggested she go to a certain area where the ground had a yellow, clay-like texture. He told her to dig up the roots of a particular plant. After boiling and steeping its roots in water, she was to dump the brown infusion into a tub of very hot water.

She followed his instructions. After I climbed into the tub she added more hot water until she was no longer able to keep her finger in it.

It did not bother me at all. Each evening I soaked in this hot bath for about thirty minutes. My health slowly improved bit-by-bit.

I, along with other village friends, had been invited to a wedding ceremony two hundred and fifty miles away in Craiesti. However, I could not attend, but my friends went.

• • •

In those days of large gatherings, pastors never wasted the opportunity to preach the Gospel. So, a wedding which normally lasted thirty minutes or so lasted three to four hours. The bride and groom had to wait until the sermon was done.

• • •

My friends informed Pastor Doja I had a life-threatening sickness that had already lasted for two and a half months. He asked all those in attendance to join him in prayer for my healing. Once they finished praying, he shared a vision he had: he saw me walking behind a wagon in a military uniform. His interpretation: I would live.

Once my friends returned home, one of them came and encouraged me, adding he expected me to already be out of the bed. This word cheered me greatly.

My health had been restored, and I was completely well within two weeks. My life went back to normal. I tailored in the village and helped my father as needed.

Soon after, my father and the other landowners in the village gave up the fight, and released their land to the collective. The year had taken a great toll on my father: almost losing me, losing the land. I saw the effect on him—he had aged before my eyes. All he had worked for, gone. It broke him.

One of my sisters and her husband in Tarnaveni needed my help to complete an important carpentry job, and my father told me I should go. It took a couple months.

On the train back home I sat across from a passenger who was sick with the flu, and continuously coughed and sneezed in my direction. When I arrived home, my father was working in the yard. He was filled with joy at my homecoming—he grabbed, hugged, and kissed me, as is common in our culture.

I came down with the flu a few days later, and recovered quickly. My father, however, became very ill. He was already weak and had no resistance. We called for the doctor, but he wanted 600 *lei* to treat my father.

We had no money and no way to get any. We had lost the land and already sold everything possible. No one in the village was in a position to help us. People simply tried to survive.

I received the order to report for active duty a little over two weeks after my father fell ill. He lost his final battle three days later. The year was 1959.

He had been a strong man in all ways: spirit, faith, and character, and he never shied away from hard work. By his actions and words, he taught his children how a husband should treat his wife, and how a father should love and instruct his children.

He had resisted surrendering the land to the Communist government as long as he could—eleven years. Sacrifice was nothing new to him. He was a hero to me.

According to Romanian custom and law, the dead are to be buried no sooner and no later than the third day. I was required to report for duty the same day as my father's funeral, and could not ignore the threats issued against me. So, I packed my bags the day of the funeral, and prepared to leave once it was over.

It tore at my heart to leave my mother and sisters. With the loss of my father, I was the only male left in the family. I felt a keen responsibility to care for them.

Once the service was over, I prepared to leave for the train station. My mother and sisters, along with many who had attended the funeral, surrounded me, sobbing. Especially my mother; she knew the threat against my life. Neither of us knew when, or if, I would return.

The two pastors who officiated at my father's funeral—Pastor Floria and Pastor Plesa—lived in the same city as the military headquarters, Medias, seventy-five miles away. They ended up on the same train as me.

Of course, they were aware of my situation, so during the trip they advised me not to present myself until the next day. Romania had a law: when a death occurred in a family, there was a one-day grace period for reporting. The regional pastor invited me to spend the night at his house, which I did.

The next morning when I reported for duty, I faced the same captain from the prior year. I tried to explain my father had passed away, and the funeral had been the day before. He was furious.

"You were supposed to be on the train that left last night at 11:00 PM."

I then understood why the other young men from my village had not been called to report. The captain had planned to make good on his threat. The train I missed had been filled with young men judged to be criminals, headed to work in the Danube region project. The captain made it clear if I showed up late again, I was to go straight to jail.

Amazed and deeply grateful for God's protection, I rejoiced on the train ride home.

My mother did not see me until I opened the door.

"Mother, God did a wonderful—"

"Praise the Lord!" she shouted as she lifted her hands.

She wrapped me in her arms. Her sorrow turned to joy. A son she thought might be lost was safe. We knew God had protected me, and we gave Him many thanks.

I filled the following year by helping my mother and working as a tailor.

One day a deputy from the local police station approached me, and told me I was to report immediately to the military headquarters in Medias. Again, none of the other young men from the village had been called up. He added the commander of the local police station had received the orders, but put them in his pocket and forgot to get them to me.

I reported the next day. The same captain from the two previous times flew into another tirade. He yelled, screamed, cursed, and threatened me once again. For thirty minutes I sat and listened. I tried to explain what had happened.

"Captain, I shouldn't even be here today. I haven't seen or received an order. I was notified last night by a deputy to report immediately, so I came. How can I be blamed when I have no order?"

He launched into another litany of threats. However, I was free to go.

Again, as before, once I returned home we celebrated with deep thanksgiving. God had spared me from certain suffering.

In my heart I always wondered if the local police commander neglected to give me the order because he knew of the threat. Regardless, God knew.

CHAPTER 6

STELA

He who finds a wife, finds a good thing . . .
— Proverbs 18:22, NASB

I HAD BARELY SET DOWN my bag when my mother noticed me.

"Nelu, oh praise God."

This little bit of a woman ran and grabbed me around the waist. She buried her face into my chest as her tears flowed. Pentecostals are known for our loud rejoicing, and rejoice we did. I am certain at least one neighbor heard it.

Of course, we were happy I was home safe and secure. Yet, the question hung over us: for how long? We knew the call would come.

Would God step in again to protect me?

We trusted so.

I continued to live with my mother and two sisters, and worked as a tailor and in our fields to help my mother pay the taxes on our home. Almost two years passed before the order to report came. I was twenty-five.

This time, all the young men with whom I had originally been called had also been told to report. Much to my relief the captain who had threatened me three different times had been removed from his office.

We were trucked to a farm in the southwestern part of Romania to work. There was no boot camp, no training to become a soldier. They needed field-hands. That was the common practice since the government was not able to recruit laborers to work the fields on a consistent basis.

That particular farm covered approximately one thousand acres. Three to four hundred soldiers were brought in to the work the crops. No farm equipment was available, so everything was done by manual labor as in years gone by. The crops were corn and wheat.

Upon arrival at the farm, we were asked what skills we possessed. The officers mentioned a need for a tailor, so I raised my hand. I was put in charge of not only the officers', but also the soldiers' uniforms.

The men had only one uniform and one extra shirt. Damaged uniforms were brought to me each night for repair so they were able to be worn the next morning. I slept during the day in one of the makeshift barracks.

After nearly a month, they needed someone to cut hair, so I volunteered. I had never cut hair before, but I figured I could do it as well as anyone else. Working at night allowed me to help with the cooking. There were no restrictions regarding how much food I ate, so at times I shared it.

When the young men from our village wrote home, they told their families what I was doing, and how much they appreciated it. Those months passed quickly and were not bad at all.

My time in the military was short, just three months because of my age. The service requirement was two years, but not beyond age twenty-six. After getting out, my sister, Leontina, and her husband, who lived in Blaj, asked me to help them build a home. I stayed with them to help with the carpentry. We converted one of the rooms at the end of the house into living quarters for me as compensation.

I also got a job as a tailor in a reputable tailoring shop. This was one of the times when having friends or family in high places was a huge benefit to me. One of my cousins was the mayor of Blaj at the time of my move.

Everyone was required to have an identification card to show where they were born or lived at the time of the Soviet takeover. If a person lived in a village such as I did, the government's leaders wanted to keep the individual there. A person could not move to the city or get a job there.

It was considered illegal for the manager of any business or co-op, which was owned by the government, to hire anyone aside from local residents. This kind of restriction of movement made it easier for the Securitate to keep track of people. There was freedom of travel within the borders, but no freedom to change residence.

Of course, if a person had enough money, he or she was able to go to the office where identification cards were given to obtain a new card. Money always talked, and so did connections.

• • •

My current pastor, Pastor Lazar Gog, tells the story of trying many times to get approval to move his wife and children from where they lived in Cluj to where he pastored in Ploiesti. Every

time he entered Romanian Pentecostal Church as his employ-
ment on the application. Every time, he was denied because he
was a Christian.

Finally, he wrote the initials RCP as his employer; he was approved. They thought his entry meant Romanian Communist
Party.

• • •

I was hired after a few months by a large furniture company to
work in its upholstery department. My job was to fill in, wherever
needed, on the assembly line. I learned the forty-one-step uphol-
stering process.

After some months they put me in charge of the department
that made the patterns and sewed the materials. Having been a tailor made it quite easy for me.

One day, the head engineer of the company stormed over
to me.

"Muntean, I just found out you aren't a member of the United
Communist Youth (UCY). I'm sending the secretary in right away
to sign you up. If you don't join, I'll have to fire you."

I had a decision to make: lose my job or join the UCY. I wanted
no part of weekly Communist meetings, so when the secretary
came in I asked her every question possible, hoping to figure a way
to avoid doing it.

In her defense, she was direct with her answers. She assured
me at the indoctrination meeting no one asked me any questions.
I simply paid the membership fee and received my identification
card. All I needed to do was attend regular meetings. Reassured

the meetings were nothing more than a formality—no actions of support or involvement was required—I decided not to jeopardize my job.

The first meeting was interesting. I did not understand a single point of the report the secretary read. Once finished, she asked for questions or comments, as was required.

Since I had not understood any portion of the report, I asked a lot of questions, and requested a copy of the report. The secretary acted flustered and embarrassed because she had no answers for me. Later she came over to me.

"You made me look bad, so please don't come to anymore of our meetings. I'll mark your name as having attended and no one will know the difference."

"Thank you, I won't come again."

Embarrassing her had not been my intention, but I was more than happy to accommodate her request. That was the total effort of anyone trying to get me to join the Communist Party.

The military behind me and gainfully employed, it was time to think about getting married. I had enjoyed the company of young ladies, so I had a pretty good idea what I wanted in a wife.

Evidently, the older women of my church thought it was time for me to settle down as well. They always tried to match me with available young women. I grew tired of the help, as kindly as it was meant.

I had definite priorities. First, I wanted my future wife to be a Christian, preferably a Pentecostal, since that was my faith. My mother, of course, felt the need to encourage me to get a strong woman in stature and character. She said I needed someone who was able to work by my side, bear children, and was healthy. She always was a wise woman.

Shortly after I had gotten out of the military, I was invited to a wedding in Brasov. Without my knowledge, Pastor Popovici had played matchmaker. When I arrived at the wedding he told me about a young woman in attendance, an accountant, who seemed to impress him. Someone he thought might interest me.

His meddling made me want to leave immediately after the ceremony. I told my friend that was exactly what we would do, and leave we did once the wedding was over. We left for the train station. When Pastor Popovici realized I had left, he got into his car and came to talk us into returning for the reception. He told me it was very embarrassing for him for me to leave. Reluctantly, we agreed to go back.

Once we returned, I found I had been seated next to her, and we had been seated next to the bride and groom. Everyone who congratulated the happy couple then turned to us, and asked us when we were getting married. Needless to say, I left as soon as possible.

The pastor called me to talk about the girl. I let him know I did not need a wife to count my money; I was able to do it. I wanted a wife able to work by my side.

He responded, "There's a young woman who lives in Sighisoara whose father, Zaharia, is the pastor over six churches. They're a very good family. The family's name is Apahidean."

I did not want to be rude, so I thanked him for the information. I did not think about it again.

The Pentecostal community was not huge at that time, so it was not uncommon to travel great distances for weddings. Everyone knew each other. With the constant pressure of daily living under the Communist system, the opportunity to celebrate a wedding together was a joyful event, a chance for the young unmarried people to meet each other.

Once a young woman turned seventeen or eighteen, thoughts turned to possible husbands. Not only was the young woman thinking along these lines, but her family members were as well.

Such was the case of the young woman who became my bride. She rejected her brother's offering of young suitors and prayed for God to choose her husband.

"Lord, you know my future, heart, soul, and the kind of man I need. So, I'm going to trust You to bring him."

It was not too long before I was invited to another wedding in the village of Seleus, where the pastor performing the wedding ceremony happened to be the father of this young lady. At the reception outside, my friend and I were standing in the side yard visiting and watching the festivities when a pretty young woman walked up. She seemed to know who I was, but I was suspicious. She smiled and extended her hand.

"Hi. My name is Steluta Apahidean."

I remembered the pastor had told me about her. We had a pleasant conversation, but I remained reserved because I thought it possible she was aware of the pastor's comments and wanted to connect with me. We parted on friendly terms, and a year passed without any communication.

One day, I received a postcard from her. It had a simple greeting and asked me how I was doing. I was surprised, but curious and cautious. I had never allowed myself to fall in love and wanted to be careful.

It took me at least three months before I answered her post-card. We spent a few weeks writing back and forth. I had definitely grown interested, but I wanted to learn more about her character, so I planned a couple of tests.

I realize the idea of tests might not be popular with some people, but marriage is a serious matter. So, I wrote and suggested we meet in a city which was between our two cities which were about ninety miles apart. A good Christian girl would never agree to such a suggestion, so I really hoped her response was no. I was not disappointed.

"No!"

She made it clear if I wanted to spend time with her, I needed to come to her home. I was very pleased. Many of the young women I knew professed strong faith, but failed to act on it. I do not judge them, but simply show why character was important to me.

In 1964, no one had a telephone in the home. However, there was a special bank of telephones at the post office. If someone wanted to make a call, the person notified the post office telephone operator to make the call at a certain time, which is what I did.

Steluta was given a receipt to let her know about the call. It was planned for 8:45 AM on the next Saturday morning. My plan was to surprise her by arriving on the train a few minutes later. I was curious to see how she handled the whole situation.

I had not planned on the train being an hour late. Steluta says she waited a long time. Once 8:45 PM had passed, she asked the post office telephone operator to check the line to Blaj.

After the line was checked, the operator—a neighbor of hers—said, "Steluta, there's nothing wrong with the line. Relax, I bet he's coming on the train."

Every few minutes, Steluta went through the same routine with the operator.

At 10:00 AM I walked through the post office door. When Steluta saw me, she ran to me, laughing and gave me a big hug.

I thought, Wow. Not only is she still waiting, but she isn't mad.

The operator laughed and said, "See, I told you he was coming. I told you he was coming by train."

I think I might have fallen in love right at that moment.

From the post office we walked to the cafeteria where we shared a bowl of ice cream. I gave her a bag of gold foil-covered chocolate coins which she dumped into her bag.

We spent the day getting acquainted. I met her big family—her father and mother, Zaharia and Anna; her six brothers; and two sisters. The next morning I went to church with Steluta and her family, and we spent the afternoon together after the Sunday meal. Our time together was enjoyable, and I hoped for more visits in the future.

Because of work, I was only able to visit Steluta every other weekend. That was okay because I did not want to rush the relationship. When I reflect back, though, one might think I did rush. I enjoyed getting to know her and her family.

When a man has chosen a woman to be his wife and the mother of his children, he should not do it carelessly or too quickly. Still, by my third trip to Sighisoara, there was no question—I loved her. Her joy of life and laughter were infectious.

That weekend, on Sunday afternoon as we walked hand-in-hand down an oak tree-lined dirt road, I stopped and asked her if I could kiss her.

A smile lit her face as she said, "Yes."

It was her first kiss.

Ana and Zaharia Apahidean. Stela's parents.

Stela as a teenager.

Stela, as little girl with her Aunt Marioara.

The home Stela grew up in.

CHAPTER 7

DELIGHT

Delight yourself in the Lord, and He will give you the desires
of your heart.
　　　　　　　　　　　　—Psalm 37:3, NASB

OUR FIRST KISS—I NEVER EXPECTED to be so blessed.

There were other girls in the community who felt it their responsibility to warn Steluta about my reputation with the ladies. What those girls did not know was during my fifth visit, I had told her about my past girlfriends, and of some of the gossip they had spread.

She did not have an issue with it which showed she was not the jealous type—another wonderful character trait.

"John, I have two ears, it goes in one and out the other. I trust you."

It was on the sixth weekend visit when I asked her to marry me. She claims I asked her father for her hand just four months after my first visit to her home, but I say it was six months. Regardless, I am grateful she pestered her brother Liviu, for my address.

Being the photographer at most of the Pentecostal weddings,

he knew me. I am also very thankful she sent me the postcard. Otherwise, we might not be married today.

Shortly after her father gave his blessing, we went to the government office to have the legal mandated wedding—a civil ceremony on July 4, 1964. Without the civil ceremony, we could not get approval for our church wedding. For us, the day that mattered, our real wedding date, was when God joined us as one on August 2, 1964.

Stela was not so different than any other young bride preparing for her wedding. She wanted a beautiful wedding dress. Back then, the Pentecostal religion in Romania taught wearing fancy clothes was a sin because the wearer might become prideful. Not even wedding rings were worn. Stela knew all this, but did not share the same convictions and was not concerned with what others thought. She talked to her father.

"Daddy, I want to wear a real wedding dress."

He answered, "Honey, you wear whatever you want. It's all right with me. Don't worry what others say."

He and Pastor Popovici were to officiate over the wedding ceremony. However, as head pastor over six regional churches, Stela's father was not concerned about the people.

After asking her father, she checked with me. I wanted her to have whatever made her happy.

There is a Romanian custom, which Pentecostals did not keep which is quite unique among world wedding traditions. First, the groom must pick up his bride to take her to the ceremony. I took a taxi out to Stela's home. The taxi driver wanted me to hurry since rain threatened to turn a dirt road into a muddy road. I arrived, ready to escort my beautiful bride to the church, but a rope was strung across the porch steps at about three feet high.

Not all of Stela's brothers knew the Lord at that time, so two of them stood barring my entrance into the house. They expected the customary bribe of wine or money.

They demanded five liters of wine; seriously. One of her brothers who was a believer began to argue with them. I took advantage of their distraction, stepped back a few feet, ran, and hurtled the rope landing on the third step. Success!

For all intents and purposes, Stela and I arrived at the church on time.

As was the custom, the wedding celebration began with a sermon. The Gospel took precedence. Pastor Popovici preached for almost two hours.

Then, he announced, "Now, the wedding begins."

I stepped up to the front and waited for Stela as she walked down the aisle. Instead of wearing the simple white shift with a white head scarf and no flowers, my bride rented a wedding dress with a train so long its weight pulled at her waist. She wore a simple veil and carried flowers. Once she reached me, she put a flower in my lapel.

Well, the idiom: it was so quiet you could hear a pin drop was not befitting, not at the time. There were audible gasps and whispers echoed throughout the crowd.

"Oh how beautiful!"

Contrary comments were also released.

"Oh no! Do you see that? That's a sin."

However, it mattered not. She was beautiful—not only on

the outside, but also on the inside. I was a blessed man. We were a happy couple.

• • •

We began our life together in Blaj, in the one room I had converted into a very small living quarter at the end of my sister's house. I had prepared it as best I could for my wife. I had turned the room into living quarters with a kitchen and living area, and a bed. Those were good times for us, in spite of the living conditions of the outside world.

Early on, we spent each weekend with my mother. We left Fridays after work, packed a picnic dinner, got on our bikes, and headed out. We stopped somewhere along the road to eat.

It was, in fact, the best of times. My wife and mother fell in love with each other. Laughter between them was the most common sound heard in the house.

It is quite amazing how people continue to survive, even in extreme times, and grab or create moments of joy. Life goes on. It was not long before we were expecting a little one.

When it became dangerous for my wife to ride her bike, our visits with my mother were less frequent. Yet together, Stela and I were happy in our little home. Our first son, Ovidiu, was born while we still lived in Blaj.

Our living quarters were so small we decided to move to Sighisoara when Ovidiu was just four months old. We turned an unfinished basement room in her parent's home into living quarters for the three of us.

The only reason we could move to Sighisoara without bribing

someone was because my wife had been born there and owned land. Many years prior to the Communist takeover, my father-in-law had purchased small plots of land side-by-side for his children. This was the custom in Romania so the family could remain close.

We were thankful for it, and decided to build a home there. Our life changed significantly when we married and started our family.

• • •

Romania had suffered severely under Gheorghiu-Dej's totalitarian rule of communism. The people starved while those within the RCP had all they wanted to eat. Thousands of tons of food were exported to fill grocers' shelves in other countries while the breadlines remained long and Romania's food shelves were empty all too often.

In *Red Horizons*, Lt. Gen. Pacepa writes much of the export began when Henry Jacober initially tried to forge the agreement for Israel to ransom Romanian Jews with Gheorghiu-Dej. It was not until Jacober offered to build an automated chicken farm, free of charge if five hundred Jewish families were allowed to leave Romania, when Dej agreed. Once he approved the plan, a modern chicken farm was built in the small village of Peris on land owned by the Ministry of Interior.

"By the end of 1964, the Ministry of Interior had become the largest meat producer in Romania. It owned chicken farms, turkey farms, and pig farms producing tens of thousands of animals a year, several cattle farms, and other farms with some 100,000 head of sheep—all with automated slaughterhouses, refrigerated storehouses, and packing plants."[9]

Yet, the people of Romania starved.

In 1965, Gheorghe Gheorghiu-Dej, supreme Communist leader of the reign of terror, died from lung cancer. Romanians had hoped for a better life. However, it was not to be. Nicolae and Elena Ceausescu came into power.

Under the Ceausescu regime, living conditions only grew worse. Grave danger lurked in the breadlines. Portions of food were allotted to each family based on its size. In order to be certain to get the family's ration it was important to get to the market early.

Stela would leave for the market around 4:00 AM in order to get a place near the front of the line. Depending on which market she shopped, it did not open until 8:00 AM or 9:00 AM. Of course, by opening time the lines were already very long.

Although most people knew each other, at times actual fist fights erupted. The greatest danger, however, came from not knowing if an informer was among nearby people.

Informing had become a way of life for many, not necessarily because they wanted to inform. Many did it simply to gain power and money, but others because they wanted to live and feed their families.

What parent wouldn't find a way to feed his or her child who cries from hunger?

One Friday on the way home from work, I went by the meat market and saw people standing in line. I stopped and asked why. I was told they heard there would be meat on Sunday.

"Meat on Sunday?"

I did not understand.

"Why are you in line, now? Are you going to stay the whole weekend?"

"We are going to take turns standing in line with different family members."

Usually, the meat consisted of bones with a few chunks of meat attached. On our way to church at 9:00 AM Sunday morning, the line held about one hundred and fifty people.

As we went by, the man at the window hollered, "No more!"

Then he closed the window. A large number of people had to turn and go home empty-handed. Sadly, this was normal. Yet, no one dared complain out loud for fear an informer might report it.

Those who cannot look to faith for strength, nor to a God whom they do not believe in for help, might think their only recourse is to work for the enemy—the government. Family members turned on each other. Neighbors turned on neighbors.

It might be easy to think, *I would never do that,* but until a person has walked daily in the valley of the shadow of death, that same person does not know what he or she would do.

Total government control was a part of daily life. The government owned everything, and the citizens worked for and were paid by them. They dictated the salary. No one was safe, all lived in some level of fear.

Always in the back of many minds was the hope the Americans would come to liberate them. They never came.

For a very short time, pressure from the government seemed to ease up. Then, our new leader, Nicolae Ceausescu, became very concerned about the declining population rate. Four of every five pregnancies ended in abortion.

Ceausescu stated the fetus in the womb belonged to the state. Abortion was outlawed unless the pregnancy was detrimental to the health of the woman or in the case of rape. All contraceptives were outlawed. There was no sex education available in the schools or elsewhere and no medical books available to the public.

Ceausescu set a goal to increase Romania's population from twenty-three million to thirty million by the year 2000. In 1967, Decree No. 770 required women under the age of forty-five to have five children, whether married or not. They were required to report monthly to the clinic for pregnancy testing.

If they carried a baby, then they were closely monitored by doctors to make certain the pregnancy carried to term. In 1967 and 1968, the birth rate doubled. Babies born in those years were called "Ceausesci" babies.

Outlawing abortion, with no birth control available, created a challenge. The mortality rate for women seeking illegal abortions exploded. The lack of proper nourishment and medical care caused underweight babies. If a baby was born and weighed less than three and a half pounds, the baby was not given any medical care.

If the baby lived, so be it. If the baby died, so be it. The requirement was to have another, and another. Women continued to die.

Stela and I welcomed each of our children as the gifts from God they were. Except for some health issues my wife suffered, we would have had more than the five we were blessed with. No one dared called them "Ceausescu" babies around me.

Stela and John's wedding picture, August 1964.

CHAPTER 8

STRAIGHT PATHS

*Trust in the Lord with all your heart, and do not lean on
your own understanding.
In all your ways acknowledge Him, and He will make your
paths straight.*
—Proverbs 3:5–6, NASB

SIGHISOARA, WITH A POPULATION OF approximately thirty-five thousand people, is located in the region of Transylvania. It is the birth city of a very famous man in history—King Vlad "the Impaler" Dracula, born in 1431. The Impaler was a name he came by legitimately, as it was his favorite way to punish his enemies—even perceived enemies.

The bodies or heads of those he punished were displayed on large stakes by the side of the roads as a warning to all who thought to resist. Legend has it he murdered forty thousand people who opposed him—all ages, sexes, and political persuasion. One has to wonder if the spirit of violence, murder, and torture lived in the land waiting for those of the twentieth century—who became experts.

Sighisoara is one of the oldest cities in Romania; it was built in the late twelfth century. It is a beautiful city where the new is mixed with century's old structures, including the house Count Dracula was born in which is now a restaurant in the Fortress on the hill.

Fortunately, Stela's parents allowed us to turn the single basement room of their home into living quarters while we built our home. We brought our stove, furniture, and all our belongings to set up house.

I went to the co-op to find a job. In the United States, a parent company might have a lot of subsidiaries. In a Communist country, the government owns and controls every aspect of business.

There were three cooperatives in Sighisoara. The co-ops controlled all the shops in the city, and all work came through it. I chose to find work through Prestarea Cooperative of Sighisoara.

When I went to the headquarters and told them of my trade experience, they sent me to an upholstery shop where four men worked. For some reason, the head man did not want me in the shop; I do not know what he feared.

Prestarea did not want me to go to work for one of the other upholstery shops, so they set me up in a small building—a shop which was mine. They supplied me with orders and materials with which to complete the jobs. I worked by myself. The salary I received from the cooperative was meager at best, but we survived.

It was January 1966 when I made application to build a home on the parcel of land owned by my wife which was protected by the inheritance laws. The property, which was in her name, was no larger than a quarter acre. It was legal for her to build a house on the land.

We assumed we would receive approval, and dug the basement. We were fortunate to obtain enough bricks from a torn down furnace which we planned to use for the basement walls.

I had worked alone until March when a crisis erupted in the other upholstery shop. They had received a special order to work on six armchairs. These were not just ordinary chairs, but beautiful chairs with sculpted lion's heads on the armrests and lion's paws for the feet. The chairs were to be covered in leather which was not easy to come by at all.

The other shop, however, had destroyed the materials provided by the client. The mayor of Sighisoara, Mr. Bolindut, personally oversaw the project. He brought Mr. Grabcev, the president of the co-op, to my shop to explain the situation, and to ask me to help. I told them yes, but I needed someone who knew how to sew leather plus an industrial sewing machine.

The chairs had to be done within two weeks. An ordinary citizen would not have a chance to obtain any of the needed materials, but the leather arrived in short order.

Mr. Bolindut checked the project's progress every day. It was during this time I received a response to my application to build. It had been denied. The parcel of land was three hundred and ninety feet outside the city limits. To say I was upset was putting it mildly.

My mood evidently showed on my face because when the mayor came by, he asked, "John, what's wrong? You look upset."

I had not planned on saying anything, but handed him the refusal.

"How can I be happy with this response? All I wanted to do was build a house for my family."

He looked at it and said, "Leave everything as it is, and come with me."

We walked a short distance to the planning office and right into the head engineer's office. The man behind the desk jumped to his feet to welcome us. Mr. Bolindut handed him the paper and asked why my application had been denied.

After he looked over the paper, he answered, "It's outside the city limits. However, he can build his house, and then receive only a small fine."

"No! If he builds without approval, and there is a catastrophe, he won't be covered by insurance. On my order you're to extend the city limits to include their parcel. I want all the documents in my office within two days for my signature. Then you're to personally deliver the approval to Mr. Muntean."

The reality is, if I had not been necessary, I would not have received my approval for construction.

The head engineer saluted and said, "Understood."

On the second day, he came to my shop and gave me the approval.

The mayor was very pleased the chairs were delivered on time, since it had been on his shoulders to get the job done for the regional officials in Brasov. My years of working—not only as a tailor, but also in the upholstery factory—prepared me for all the work that came my way. Evidently, my work was viewed as superior, so I began to receive preferential treatment.

Let me be clear on this, my value to the party rested only in my ability to deliver what the party required. In my mind, I knew it was God's favor resting on me for His plan and purpose for my life.

At that time, there were three men placed in positions of authority who not only proved to be a blessing to me, but also to the quality of life in Sighisoara. Things were better there compared to what others suffered in other parts of the country.

One of the benefits of my newfound favor with the Sighisoara Party leadership was the approval of my construction loan financing by the co-op, as well as the use of the cooperative's construction crew. I wanted a well-built house able to withstand weather extremes.

All the walls, interior and exterior, were built from specially-made bricks which had been hand-formed by a gypsy who baked them until they were red throughout. Once the bricks were dried and cleaned the construction crew went to work.

Once winter came, all work stopped until the following spring. Finally, the walls and roof were on, and Stela and I took over. It was time for the interior work. We looked forward to transforming the shell of a house into a home.

There is something more to tell of this story, but I will revisit it. For now, it is important to share how God blessed me with a strong, faithful wife. Although great with child and busy caring for another eleven-month-old, my sweet wife worked by my side as much as possible.

Stela stayed at home with our son, Ovie. Most of her days began with a two-mile walk at four in the morning to stand in the breadline. There were three markets which divided up food items: the bread market, the sugar-flour-oil market, and the meat market.

The meat market is where bones were found: soup bones, rib bones, all kinds of bones with a little bit of meat attached. The roasts, steaks, and chops were exported out of the country, except for what filled the special warehouses which only long-time members of the Communist Party, or those of high rank, drew from.

Most of the food consumed by the citizens came from their gardens and the poultry they raised. What they did not have—fruit, cheeses, and different kinds of produce—were traded for or purchased at the swap meets.

Oftentimes, Stela walked back into town to search the markets for any leftover foods, like butter or salami. It was not unusual for her to come home empty-handed.

Once, a drunkard went to the swap meet in our city to buy a pig. Only the head or legs were available, so he purchased the head, put it on a table, and began to hit it with a stick.

He yelled, "I'm going to beat you until you tell me where the rest of your body is."

He thought he was making a joke. It was assumed the rest of the pig had been exported, so the man was arrested for making a political statement.

• • •

Many times my father-in-law came downstairs to visit with us once work was completed. I loved to hear his stories of when he was a young preacher.

One of my favorites was about when he met Christ while a soldier in the Romanian Cavalry. His life was never the same. He earned the name crazy Zaharia because of his enthusiasm for Christ.

Then, in his early years as a young husband and father, he

traveled on bicycle throughout three-fourths of Romania to preach and evangelize. At times, he was arrested and held overnight by the local police. Since they, too, were Romanians, he never suffered rough treatment.

At one point during these travels, he experienced the hand of God make provision for him like he had never seen. He had been sent out to mediate between two factions within a church. In order to make his neutrality clear, he did not take meals or stay with any of them. Instead, he slept in the open. The process took longer than he had anticipated, and he ended up going several days without food.

Exhausted and famished, he headed for home. He stopped at the top of a large hill by the side of the dirt road and had a heart-to-heart with God as he gazed down into the valley.

"Father, if I'm to continue to serve You, I need You to provide for me or I may die right here."

After his simple prayer, something caught his eye. Down the hill about two miles, on the small bridge which crossed a creek, something flashed bright and reflected the sun.

How could something that far away possibly catch my eye?

He watched for a bit as a few wagons passed over the bridge, but no one else seemed to notice the object. Curiosity finally convinced him to get on his bike and ride down to it. It turned out to be a valuable coin, worth enough for him to go into the next village and purchase a satisfying meal. He slept well that night.

Another time, while away from his family, Stela's father experienced a deep sense of foreboding. With no way to check, since there was no electricity or telephones, he decided to immediately push toward home.

As he rode into his village and passed the cemetery, he saw a freshly dug gravesite. When he arrived home, his wife wore a black dress. They had lost their third child, two-and-a-half-year-old Minerva. His beautiful little girl who loved her daddy, had died from a bad reaction to the polio vaccination.

His trips were never as long afterwards.

Zaharia's extensive travels throughout Romania proved to be a blessing once he became involved with the underground church movement several years after Stela and I were married. He and his son, Liviu, were responsible for Bibles and Christian literature secretly spread throughout the country. They were never caught. Had they been, they would have been sent to prison without hesitation.

He loved having us around; he often offered to spend time with our son, Ovidiu, while Stela and I worked on finishing the house. He was a great man of God, a powerful example to all, and I loved him as my father.

• • •

In spite of the Constitution's guarantee of religious freedom, it was illegal to receive or purchase a Bible anywhere in Romania. This is why Zaharia's and Liviu's work years later was worth such a risk.

When I received a Bible in the mail from Germany on my thirtieth birthday, I was amazed. It was hand-delivered in a box by the mailman. Before this, I had the New Testament, but not a complete Bible.

What a blessing!

Why the mail was not opened at the border as all mail was known to be, I do not know, but God does. There were so many ways God's hand of protection was upon us. Had the mailman guessed what was inside and reported it, I could have been arrested, regardless of my innocence.

Fear was the greatest weapon used by the secret police. Without warning, they might break in to search homes—day or night—on the pretext of finding something illegal or anti-government. There was no requirement for a search warrant.

Thankfully, we never suffered such a violation of privacy. Instead, the Lord allowed us opportunities to study His Word together as a family.

Ovidiu,
the first born and first son.

Johnny, 2nd child and 2nd son. Died at age 3 ½.

Liviu, as a baby.

Tabita.

Danny, the youngest child.

John and Stela's home
after first flood in 1970.

CHAPTER 9

GRIEF AND COMFORT

Blessed are those who mourn, for they shall be comforted.
—Matthew 5:4, NASB

EARLIER, I ALLUDED TO THE rest of the story as Stela and I finished our home. It is time to tell you about our Nelucu. Little Johnny was born on August 17, 1966. He was a strapping nine-pound baby with blond hair, long curling eyelashes, and dark brown eyes.

He was healthy in every way. It was a joy to see his first smile and hear his first giggle and encourage his early efforts to hold on and stand in our laps.

We experienced warm weather into early October 1966, for which we were very grateful. It gave us more time to get the bricks clean in order for them to be used for the walls.

One nice afternoon, Stela and Ovie, who was a year and a half, spent several hours working on the bricks. My wife worked hard while Ovie played at her side. Johnny slept in the baby stroller, tucked in snugly.

We first noticed something was not quite right with Johnny when Stela tried to feed him. Up to this point, Johnny had been a good eater. That evening, however, he refused to eat anything, except for a small amount of milk. Over the next two days, Johnny suffered from fever, vomiting, and diarrhea. On the fourth day, my wife took him to the hospital.

Johnny was admitted and Stela stayed with him. The doctor diagnosed Johnny with the flu. The only prescribed treatment was to feed him mashed carrots. Stela nursed him, but he could not hold it down.

The children's hospital had a dorm room for the mothers to sleep in—twelve beds with no curtains for privacy separated them. Stela slept there at night and spent her days in the rocking chair next to Johnny's bed.

My wife continually asked questions about his condition. The staff doctor did not seem concerned. His answer was always the same: Johnny suffered from diarrhea. Within three to four days the vomiting and diarrhea ceased, but they kept him a couple more to be certain he was over his illness.

Once home, Stela was very careful about what she fed him. Johnny was not the normal, healthy three-and-a-half-month-old he had been before. His appetite never fully returned, and within a couple months we began to notice other problems.

At first we thought the slight change was simply due to his slow recovery. His muscle tone and strength were weak. He should have developed like other babies his age—rolling over, sitting up, and eventually pulling himself up in his crib. Johnny never did any of these things, and, in time, he winced as though in pain, though he never cried out.

He continued to refuse food no matter what Stela tried to feed him. An occasional tic affected one side of his face. He was no longer able to grab fingers, hold tightly, or push his legs to stand up in my lap. His limbs lost total strength until—after months—there was no voluntary movement. He had complete feeling, but no movement.

In the beginning, we hoped his sickness had only slowed his development, but as we watched, we knew better. We did what we always did: we prayed for God to touch him and make him healthy.

My father-in-law came, anointed Johnny with oil, and prayed for his return to good health. This became his habit every time he visited. We put our faith and hope in God to help our son . . . and we waited.

At about ten months old, Johnny began to experience very small seizure-like upper body movements. Johnny could not move his arms or legs, so his shoulders tensed and drew up—almost to his ears—as he strained and grimaced.

My wife, pregnant again at this time with our third son, Liviu, insisted the nurse come to our home for the monthly state-required pregnancy wellness check. The nurse asked questions about Johnny and wrote a report about each visit.

No one in the medical field seemed concerned. We had to have answers, so we decided to take him to the specialist at the children's hospital in Targu Mures, about fifty miles away. The doctor quizzed Stela thoroughly regarding her health and nutrition during her entire pregnancy and delivery.

He took extensive notes about Johnny's well-being in the

months prior to his illness as well as everything that had happened up to that point. They cut a piece of his muscle from his left leg's calf in order to check the amount of fluid in the tissue, and they took blood from his arm. Stela stayed overnight with Johnny to hear the test results the next day.

In 1968, Communist Romania offered very limited avenues of treatment for severe illness. The specialist sat down with my wife and explained the test on Johnny's muscle tissue and blood tests proved inconclusive.

The x-rays of his brain showed brain damage. Johnny had contracted a form of pneumococcal meningitis. The doctor told my wife the degree of damage and the amount of fluid created pressure on his brain was that so severe Johnny most likely would not live past four years of age.

He looked at my wife with compassion and said, "Mrs. Muntean, there's no hope for Johnny."

She was given no papers of any kind to bring home. It was a long, lonely, and painful bus ride.

Pneumococcal meningitis is the most common form of meningitis, and is the most serious form of bacterial meningitis. At particular risk are children under age two and adults with a weakened or depressed immune system. Persons who have had pneumococcal meningitis often suffer neurological damage ranging from deafness to severe brain damage.

We did the only thing we knew to do; pray for God to heal Johnny. It is not easy to walk out this kind of faith. Stela would pray and cry, pray and cry. Some days were better than others.

I worked all day, but she took care of every need Johnny had.

He continued to grow in length like any little boy, but bit by bit he lost weight due to his refusal to eat normal amounts of food. His health continued to fail.

Although he could not talk, we never doubted his intelligence. He knew what he wanted, and he made it clear if he did not want people in his room. He made a high-pitched keening. The only people he liked nearby were his mother; grandfather; older brother, Ovie; and me.

It is not easy for any parent to see a child suffer. As a man, I felt helpless not being able to help my son beyond praying and trusting God. Inside, the pain was immense.

Our third son, Liviu, was born in March 1968. With lots of black hair and big, watchful eyes, Liviu was a large boy and quite tall for his age. In the fall of that year, we finished the house and moved in.

Shortly afterwards, a nurse Stela was acquainted with and respected, came from the government to begin a file on Johnny. She filled page after page with the information my wife provided. She seemed especially interested in finding out how my wife was able to take care of two-year-old Johnny and his two brothers so close in age.

Finally, Stela asked, "Why are you asking all these questions?"

The nurse answered, "The government is concerned that caring for Johnny is too much for you, and they want to help. You have two other healthy children who need you."

"I'm perfectly capable of caring for Johnny. No one can give him the same good care as me." Stela said suspiciously.

"I understand, Mrs. Muntean, but it really would be easier for you to care for your other children if you didn't have Johnny to care for. The government has a special sanitarium for children with handicaps."

"No, I don't want to do that," my wife said adamantly.

Had the nurse, who was an acquaintance, not trusted Stela she would never have admitted what she did.

"I don't know if this is true, but I hear they do experiments on the handicapped or disabled children like Johnny."

My wife was horrified.

"I won't let them take Johnny."

"Stela, they might come and take him forcibly."

• • •

The threat of the state taking Johnny was real. We personally knew two families who had experienced their disabled children's removal from their home.

When the revolution in 1989 finally put an end to the rule of Nicolae and Elena Ceausescu, the world was horrified and sickened by the inhumane conditions of the country's orphanages. Between one hundred thousand and two hundred thousand children filled these dilapidated buildings. They were found malnourished and starving. Children, even up to three years old were found in urine-soaked crib beds, most still not knowing how to walk. Only custodial care was given.

The orphanages housing children with disabilities were even worse. Animals received better care. Researchers found horrifying living conditions and wide-spread abuse. These orphanages were often situated in remote areas of the country to keep the embarrassing sight of disabled children away from public view.

Of course, at this time in Johnny's life we knew nothing about the conditions in the state-run orphanages. The specialist had told us Johnny most likely would not live much beyond the age of four, but we never gave up hope. We continued to pray and trust.

We asked God to either heal Johnny or keep the state from taking him from us. The thought of him being pulled from our home was unthinkable. We fought to keep fear from taking hold.

After a year of ceaseless prayer, God did, in fact, heal our three-year-old. On November 6, 1969, very early in the morning, Nelucu passed from this life into a life with Jesus, filled with love, joy, and peace. He had contracted pneumonia the week before; the doctor who attended Johnny let Stela know the time was near. Johnny, at last, was able to run free and sing God's praises with the other children in heaven.

It may be only a parent who has lost a child who knows the true depth of pain another parent experiences. The only comfort is he or she will meet his or her child again. There is nothing else like it.

A couple months prior to Johnny's passing, my wife and her mother had attended a church service where Stela was given a prophetic word from God.

"Young woman you are in a black dress, soon I will remove it."

At the time of Johnny's death, we were unaware she already carried the gift of another new life in its earliest stages.

CHAPTER 10

FAVOR

And let the favor of the Lord our God be upon us;
and do confirm for us the work of our hands . . .
—Psalm 90:17, NASB

THE DEVASTATING FLOOD OF 1970 covered thirty-seven of the thirty-nine Romanian counties, and lasted from May 12 into mid-June. Within twelve days of the initial flooding in the northern area, raging waters poured into the river behind our home which sat between the river and raised train tracks. Twenty-nine homes along our road were in its path.

We rushed to get as much of our possessions into our attic as possible. The daughter of some dear friends had come to stay with us, and she helped get the two boys to safety. Then, Stela, Susanna, and I worked as a team—my wife standing in the attic, Susanna on the steps, and me in the house as I handed Susanna the items to lift up to Stela.

By the time we moved our clothing and materials for all our upholstery and tailoring orders into our attic, any chance for escape was lost. Water rushed into the house and over my shoes. As I climbed the ladder, the water swirled around and rose fast.

The five of us were trapped—the attic had no exit. My wife was six-months pregnant with our only daughter, Tabita. We waited and listened.

The water rose and the sun set. In a short matter of time, the electrical plant went black. Soon, the only light we saw out of the small attic window glowed from a distant hill. Flashes of lighting brightened the sky while rolls of thunder rumbled over our heads. Still, the water continued to rise.

We joined hands and prayed: "Father, we trust You to protect us. You are in total control, and we ask You to give us peace."

I encouraged the children to go to sleep and told them God's guardian angels stayed busy in these situations. All of us, except Stela, fell asleep. However, before I dozed off we heard the neighboring houses break apart—roofs were torn off, and pieces of wood, trees, and brush slammed into the sides of our home.

Screams for help rang in our ears. Stela's parents lived a short distance away, and we did not know if they were safe.

The water continued to rise. People died.

The decision to build our home on a three-foot foundation and put in twelve-foot ceilings proved to be providential. The water continued to rise through the night up to one foot below our ceiling. Finally, morning came; the water appeared to be lower.

I looked out of the small attic window and saw total devastation. Of the twenty-nine homes around us, only five remained, including ours and Stela's parents. All night and most of the next day, we waited to descend from the attic.

When it was safe, we stepped down into several inches of water and nearly eighteen inches of mud. A young man named Otto, who had rescued people in his boat throughout the night, helped us to safety. Unfortunately, Otto lost his father in the flood.

Statistics state in the first twelve days, a total of two hundred and thirty villages and small towns were hit, forty-one thousand homes were destroyed, and two hundred and nine people were killed. Of course, the country experienced high numbers of animal and crop loss. A people already faced with lack of food suffered all the more.

It took two months to make the house livable again. Suzanna, the fourteen-year-old daughter of friends, proved to be a true blessing. Although Stela and I thanked God that Johnny was safe with Him, grief had wrapped its arms around my wife to the degree I knew we needed help. Suzanna had come to live with us shortly after Johnny's death. She stayed with us until her marriage at age twenty-six.

Born soon after we settled back into our home, our beautiful daughter, Tabita, with her big brown eyes and giggles, brought us great joy. Her brothers were captivated by her. As her daddy, I thought her to be the most beautiful baby in all of Romania.

Her mother began to heal.

• • •

Before the flood, my father-in-law had asked me to take the position of administrator of the church which included overseeing the church's finances. Even with so little, people still gave to the Lord as they could. I was well aware, however, how quickly people turned to gossip and cast doubt about the person responsible for finances. I wanted no part of it.

Stela and I had agreed from the very beginning of our marriage no matter what our finances looked like, we were committed tithers . . . and tithe we did. Reluctantly, I told my father-in-law I needed to pray and seek God's wisdom about what job God wanted me to do.

Each night during my prayers, I asked God for wisdom. Months passed with this same prayer on my lips. One night, I woke to the sound of my bedroom door opening. Facing the door, I saw two brilliant figures enter. Jesus was first. Our eyes locked. Even if I had wanted to, I could not have looked away.

He was the most beautiful man I had ever seen, and his eyes glowed bronze. He and the other man walked toward my bed until Jesus stopped and stood next to me. He still gazed directly into my eyes.

"John, every night you ask me for wisdom. What I give you, you use only for yourself. Use what I give you for others, and I will give you more."

At that point, both figures backed out the door. Jesus and I never broke eye contact, so I have no idea who accompanied him.

• • •

As a young girl, Stela had her own experience with the Lord. On a nightly basis, Stela's father gathered his children around to tell them about the heroes from the Bible.

Once, after he shared how the serpent tempted Adam and Eve, six- year-old Stela said, "I want to twist his neck and kill that devil."

Alarmed, her father said, "Oh no, you don't talk like that."

As a pastor, he knew the danger of certain words.

Then, at nine and a half, Stela had a vision of the devil at the side of her bed in the form of an iridescent coiled snake which changed colors from green to grey and back. The snake flicked its tongue and hissed at her. She covered her head with her blankets, but it did not stop the glow of the snake from showing through her covers.

For a solid month, it came every night. Every night, she hid from it and cried herself to sleep. She told no one because she was afraid whoever she told might think she had done something wrong to cause the devil to come to her.

One month, and she finally she cried out.

"Oh Jesus, I give you my heart, I give you my life, my soul, everything!"

At that moment, an explosion of brilliant light emanated from the far corner of her room and filled it. She saw the face of Jesus. Peace washed over her—sweet, sweet peace—and she fell asleep, never again to be visited by the serpent.

These experiences with Jesus are what grounded our faith and trust in God, especially during the flood.

• • •

During the time of the home repair, I opened a shop at my house. Over the previous years, my reputation had grown due to my specialized work. Customers went to the co-op and requested me by name. Even though I worked from home, the government continued to pay my salary. In time, the mounting work orders required the need for employees; thus, problems arose.

The leaders of the cooperative and I butted heads. They thought the manual labor cost charged to cover the three men and four women who worked through my shop needed to be lowered. Prestarea wanted a bigger bite of the apple. I was the one who set my employees hourly wages.

"No problem, as long as you lower the retail price equally."

"That's impossible," the co-op's representative refused, not happy with me.

"I'll not lower their wages. They work hard and deserve to be paid."

He threatened, "We'll take this new order and give it to one of the other shops."

"Go ahead. And while you're at it, take your sign off my shop."

With two other government cooperatives calling me on a consistent basis to work for them, I was not concerned. Within a couple weeks, Prestarea came back to me with the order which had been botched by the other shop. The president of the cooperative called me in and agreed to pay the same as before for the manual labor.

He made one comment to me.

"You're a capitalist."

I told him I did not know what the word meant, but one day I might have the opportunity to learn.

• • •

A good portion of our business came from the hospital which contracted with us to make all its linens, children's pajamas, and scrubs for medical staff. We also contracted with the hotel to make all its bed sheets and pillowcases. My business which, in reality, belonged to the government grew tremendously. My skill made me valuable to the party which proved to be a blessing.

There were some jobs I was expected to do without compensation. For example, I was told to make foam-backed cloth seat covers for the vinyl seats in all the officials' cars. It seemed the Communist officials did not like sitting on the vinyl "blocks of ice" when the outside thermometer read 30 degrees below zero.

When I share stories, even now, with customers about the types of corruption I experienced under communism, I tell them my foam-backed cloth story. Procuring the needed foam and upholstery fabric proved difficult, almost impossible. Obviously, without these, all work in my shop would have ceased.

Our shop not only did repair work on sofas and armchairs, but we also built the custom-made armchairs I designed which opened up into beds for one or two people. Then, of course, there were the official's seat covers. At times, even the Prestarea Cooperative was unable to help me.

Divine Providence stepped in to help at that point. One day I received notification German Marks had been deposited in my name at the bank. Years prior, a German friend of mine had needed financial help. I loaned him 10,000 lei to help cover emigration costs back to Germany. I knew one day he would repay me, so I had not even thought about the debt.

In Romania, any possession by a Romanian citizen of either German Marks or American dollars was illegal. When I went to the bank, they provided me with a banknote for the entire amount. This bank-note was redeemable at the government's special store where they sold goods only purchasable by foreign currency or the banknotes. They required the entire amount on the note be spent at the time of redemption.

I took advantage of this blessing and bought a radio and cassette player. With the rest, I purchased coffee and Kent cigarettes. Mind you, I am not a smoker, but to the average Romanian citizen, these cigarettes did not exist. I knew their bartering power.

I needed foam to complete our project, and the only factory that had it in the entire country was located in Timisoara, four hundred miles away. When I left, I took a full carton of Kent cigarettes plus five packs. I had my ten-year-old son, Liviu, join me for the trip.

Upon arrival, I met with the director of the factory and told him what I needed.

He said, "If my father were to rise from his grave and ask me for foam, I couldn't give him one ounce . . . impossible. Besides that, the officials in Bucharest would have to approve it."

He opened a drawer in his desk and pulled out a pack of Marasesti cigarettes, and then with a shaking hand tried to pull one from the pack. No wonder his hand shook, they were the only cigarette a Romanian could get . . . and they were nasty.

I chose this moment to reach into my pocket.

"You might like this one better."

His eyes lit up as he reached for the pack to open it. After he lit the cigarette and took a deep drag, he leaned back in his chair.

He said, "Now, we can talk."

I opened my briefcase and pulled out the carton. I placed them on his desk. When he saw it, he grabbed the carton and put it in his drawer.

"Now, we don't need to talk. Go and rent the largest truck and trailer you can find and come back here. We'll load it and you can be on your way."

He called in his right-hand man and told him to show Liviu the entire factory. The cigarettes—if he had been granted access to them through the special store—would have cost him a month and a half's wages.

Once I arrived at the location to rent a truck, I was told it would be two weeks before any truck was available.

I asked, "You have no trucks at all I can rent?"

The manager shook his head.

"No. No trucks for two weeks."

Again, I reached into my pocket and grabbed two packs of cigarettes. I placed them on his desk.

With my hand still on them, I asked, "Can we resolve this problem with these?"

He raised one eyebrow.

"What kind of truck would you like?"

"The largest you have, and I want it in ten minutes."

"You'll have it in ten minutes."

And I did. It was a truck similar to those used by the military with tall sides and a tarp cover, plus an empty trailer with sides to pull behind.

Back at the foam factory, the director personally supervised the loading of the truck and trailer beds. When my order was completed, he instructed the men to overfill both. I told him I did not expect any favors, but he told me to keep my mouth shut because he knew I did not get the cigarettes for free. We covered everything with a tarp.

Those in Sighisoara, who told me I would never be able to get any foam, hounded me about how I did it. I kept my mouth shut and stored it in my home. Not too long after my trip, a furniture factory from a smaller town near us contacted me to ask for foam. I had the foam and they had the upholstery fabric which I needed, so we made the trade. It was Socialist business as usual.

• • •

Another way I butted heads with the cooperative's head man was through my opposition to the cooperative's policy for hiring and firing employees. Once an employee was fired, all that was needed was to show up at the co-op headquarters, be interviewed, and then make empty promises to improve work production. The employee then received a letter of re-instatement.

How was that incentive to do good work?

Again, I refused to comply. Again, I was called a capitalist. I guess I was, but I did not know it at that time.

There is no question my way of doing business did not line up with the Socialist agenda. They had to tolerate me because my shop was the only shop in the region to produce the type of service and goods at the quality offered. My uncompensated services to regional politicians, police, and the Securitate kept them off my back.

Whether it was the mayor's, police chief's, or the head of the secret police's office, I was well-known enough to get waved through without my identification checked when I arrived to do repair work on the furniture. All of the top Communist officials called me Muntean instead of Mr. Muntean, showing their respect and like for me. This proved to be a good thing. Yet, I did not know for what God was preparing me.

CHAPTER 11

WISDOM

But if any of you lacks wisdom, let him ask of God,
who gives to all men generously and without reproach,
and it will be given to him.

—James 1:5, NASB

IT IS A GOOD THING I sought wisdom from God because there is no way I could have readied myself for the journey ahead. I accepted the role of administrator of our church, but did not understand its impact on my future.

In 1972, due to an exceptionally rainy season, a mudslide took down the back wall of the building our church rented for services. We had no church building in which to worship, and the government had no intention of approving the purchase of another building suited for our needs.

The government's reason was simply: "We don't build or support churches." As far as it was concerned: no church eliminated problems with those Christians.

As administrator, I had the responsibility to come up with a solution. Our church had grown to approximately three hundred and fifty congregants. I met with different city officials frequently to resolve our problem to no avail. An idea finally came which I shared with my father-in-law, the senior pastor. He encouraged me to pursue it, so I did.

I put my solution in a document and made an appointment to see the Communist officer in charge of the region's churches. He headed the Ministry of Cult Commission, so anything pertaining to religious practice, service, or business passed through his office. This is how every aspect of religion in Romania was controlled.

I drove to Targu Mures to the office of Inspector Tonco, a tall blond man of Hungarian descent. He was known to me, for he had benefited from my services several times. We had already discussed the problem facing the church many times. He kept telling me it was impossible to purchase property for the church. He had given approval for our church to rent property, but he knew full well there were no places to rent.

He was not prepared for my proposal.

After a few pleasantries, he asked me why I had come. I handed him my announcement which informed him of the grand opening of four new churches, temporarily in members' homes. I sat quietly and watched his face turn bright red.

In a tightly controlled voice, he said, "I couldn't control this church community when it met in one location, how am I supposed to when you meet in four?"

"Give us your approval to purchase a property. Then, we'll be in one location and you can continue to do your job."

After additional discussion, he agreed.

"I promise I'll be supportive of your intention to purchase

property; however, you'll have to get the approval of all the officials in Sighisoara. I also need your assurance you won't tell anyone of my promised approval."

I thanked him and told him I trusted him to keep his word. It was up to me to get the agreement from the others. Thankful for the success of the visit, I needed to focus on the next task: meeting with the Sighisora officials.

Finally, all the previous years of work done without compensation paid off. I met them individually to secure their promise to approve our request. Each made me promise not to reveal their approval. None wanted the others to know. It evidenced their fear of each other, but more than that, the system.

During one of these visits, Ioan Ceanga, the municipal secretary of the Communist Party over Sighisoara, cautioned me.

"Mr. Muntean, I'll approve the purchase. However, if you share the news with your congregation and it gets out to the public, it might cause you trouble."

"Why do you say that?" I asked.

"There are those who are against you and will try to stop the purchase. I advise you to keep it quiet until everything is completed."

I promised to keep the purchase confidential. All aspects of it remained a secret from our congregation, the public, and, I suspect, from much of the Communist leadership, especially in Sighisoara.

We already knew of a property that met the church's needs. The property was owned by two Germans, a brother and sister, with a selling price of 120,000 lei. At the time a commercial company named Lemeta rented it. The company employed forty-two people and manufactured gutters for residential property. The building was perfect for our church, but we needed a way to raise the money.

After leaving Ceanga's office I wondered how we would solve the financial end of the purchase. I stopped by my father-in-law's home to discuss the issue and found two of my brothers-in-law visiting. As I shared our good news, I followed up with a question.

"How are we going to proceed?"

My father-in-law pointed his finger in a circle which indicated the four of us.

He said, "We four will buy it. Over the years I've set aside 65,000 lei for this very purpose."

His excitement shone in his face. One brother said he had 30,000 lei and the other had 15,000 lei. We only needed 10,000 lei. They all looked at me.

Stela and I owed 120,000 lei on our house, and at that time my total monthly income was a mere 1,200 lei. With the mortgage and four children, we were very careful with our money. I told them I must talk to my wife. If she agreed, I would borrow the money from a close friend I thought might have the means to help.

Stela told me if I was certain we were able to pay the loan back by the due date, she had no problem with securing the loan. In short order, the approved signatures were gathered, the money was combined, and everything was taken to the notary.

Only commercial companies used banks. Romanian citizens used what were known as check offices. Mind you, we did not write checks; everything was done with cash.

I had prepared two checks in the amount of 50,000 lei for the brother and sister owners. Another check in the amount of 20,000 lei went to the notary once all the documents were signed.

The notary who handled the transaction said, "In all my years of doing this, never has there been this easy a transaction. Everything was perfect."

The purchase of the building was a tremendous blessing. It became our property in September 1973. Our congregation was thrilled to have a place to convert into a church.

The government, which handled all rental properties, promised us possession within six months.

Unfortunately, another devastating flood hit Romania in 1974. Because of the advanced warning, Stela and I were not only able to get our clothes and important personal items into the attic, but we were also able to save all our materials for our orders and still get to safety.

Of course, cleanup took some time. During the process, a representative from the co-op came and asked me about my losses.

I shook my head and said, "I had no losses."

He blinked his eyes in surprise.

"What do you mean you had no losses? Everybody had losses."

I could have taken advantage of the situation, as I knew others were, but I did not.

"We were able to put all our materials in our attic and still get to safety. We have no losses."

Due to the flood, the city planning department changed certain city plans, so we received notification we had to wait another six months before the church was able to take possession of the property. This proved the beginning of repeated delays—years of delays, in fact.

No matter the multiple visits to the different offices, no matter how many promises were made, the delays continued without resolution. In fact, it took years to even receive permission to use the building, but God honored our obedience in the meantime.

God's Word promises if we give faithfully, He will open windows of blessings.

I began to design various pieces of furniture which proved to be very popular. The quality of the work my shop produced continued to draw many customers.

The head of the police let me know he would not interfere with the people who came to me—on the side for work—instead of going through the co-op. We filled Prestarea's orders by day, and Stela and I worked on private orders far into the night.

Our income increased from 1,200 lei a month to between 20,000–25,000 lei a month. We paid back the money we borrowed, and paid off our mortgage. The men and women who worked for us made between 3,000–5,000 lei a month—the same amount as most Communist officials.

We bought a car, a Dacai. Of course, we only drove it on the even days because the lack of gas in the country created a system of control and rationing. Only 5 percent of the population owned cars, and most of them were Communist officials.

All too often people think a lot of money will solve their problems. We had money and even went on vacations. Those trips would never have happened without the abundant blessings of God, for which we are deeply grateful. It is, however, important to me to clarify even rats can be happy if their cage is large enough, and they have enough food. It does not make them free.

• • •

For four years, almost on a daily basis, I was in and out of the different offices of the Sighisoara officials as I tried to resolve the property issues. Our congregants wanted their church. On paper we owned the property, but meetings were still held in four homes. They were tired of waiting.

One day when I delivered an armchair to the office of the general secretary of the Communist Party in Sighisoara, Comrade Danasan, he told me to have my men leave. He needed to talk to me in private. I told my men to wait outside.

He said, "Muntean, why aren't you thinking of your children's future?"

Surprised, I did not understand the reason for his comment.

I asked, "What do you mean? Everything I do is for them. I live for them."

"They'll not have any chance for a future in this country because you're a Christian."

Shocked, I was quiet for a moment, but then remembered something significant. Six months earlier, I had been called late in the evening by the CEO of the co-op to help him out. He and his head accountant had taken out-of-town guests to a restaurant where they had gotten extremely drunk.

Near the end of the evening, the CEO, Mr. Grapvec, realized they were too drunk to drive, so he called me. When I arrived, some of the men tried to get me to drink, but I told them no. At that point, Mr. Grapvec yelled at them and told them I was a Christian who did not drink. Besides, I was there to drive them.

The head accountant, who also happened to be the brother-in-law of Comrade Danasan, invited me to sit with him. He leaned in close to me.

He whispered, "John, we're both Christians—me and my brother-in-law, Danasan."

I kept quiet; he was drunk, so I did not doubt what he said. He went on.

He said, "In fact, every evening Danasan locks his doors, pulls down his shades, and drops to his knees to pray."

Remembering that conversation, I met Danasan's eyes.

"Comrade Danasan, when you lock your doors at night and you pull down your shades to kneel to pray, to whom do you pray? I believe you pray to the same God I do. The only difference is I'm not ashamed of my God, but you are."

He sat with his head lowered.

He only said, "You're free to go."

Comrade Danasan's comments were due to my continual effort to force the release of the church property to us. The Communist leadership of the city and region wanted me to stop.

The conversation caused me to start thinking about my children's futures. Everything I did was for them. I wanted them to be able to pursue their dreams. The more I thought of it, the more troubled I grew.

I had been refused further education, not only because of the government wanting my parents' land, but also because of my faith. I wanted more for my children. Not only more opportunities, but more important, I wanted freedom for them to practice their faith without fear of persecution.

• • •

While I experienced persecution through silence and bureaucracy, my son, Ovidiu, faced another brand of trouble. Ovie had his mother's strong spirit and did not always remain quiet about his faith at school. He experienced punishment and ridicule the same as I had as a boy; however, to a greater degree.

The first two years, almost on a daily basis, he was beaten up for being a Christian. I had instructed him not to start a fight; however, I had neglected to tell him he was allowed to defend himself.

Once I realized what was happening, I told him. "Son, you don't start a fight, but when someone comes at you to attack you, hit them first."

It was not like him to want to hurt someone, so when he came home and told us the story of his first experience with self-defense, we all had a good laugh. Evidently, a boy had charged Ovie and wanted to fight. So, Ovie grabbed the boy and threw him down on the soft grass instead of the hard concrete.

He said, "I didn't want to hurt him, Daddy."

In another incident, another boy began to chase Ovie up the inside steps of the school. Ovie turned and kicked him in the chest which caused the boy to roll to the bottom. The student could not catch his breath, so he was taken to the medical clinic.

Fortunately, some students came to my son's defense and told the teachers the truth about what had happened, so he was not punished. We were quite surprised and very grateful Ovie suffered no repercussions.

My son exhibited amazing musical talent. He became proficient on the piano and guitar. One afternoon, when he was nine, the school's music students performed for parents and other students.

When it was Ovie's time to play his selection on his guitar, the teacher said, "Now, the pocait will play his guitar."

The slur affected Ovie, deeply. My son walked off the stage and out the door toward home. I saw him on the street and told him to get into the car and explain why he was not in school. As he shared the reason, anger boiled inside for my firstborn son.

I drove back to the school, strode up to the teacher, and grabbed him by his lapels. Although he was taller than me, I pushed him hard against the wall and told him to never do that again to my son.

There is only one reason I was not reported to the police or Securitate: my relationship with those in authority was well-known by the community.

Always, I considered it God's favor upon me.

For the most part, the persecution of Christian students had not lessened over the years. They continued to suffer in varying degrees for their faith, throughout the country. It never stopped.

Socialist schools were the venues for many troubling things. During the first three weeks of school every year, the fifth through seventh grade students were bussed from the schools to large farms at 7:00 AM to harvest the crops. They worked until 5:00 PM.

Of course, they were not paid. My two oldest sons experienced this, even as their mother and I had as students.

The students were also required to gather medicinal herbs every day when they were in season; they were dried, and then supplied to the government. Each school had a mandated quota. The more I thought of these things, the more troubled I became. My children were sent to school to learn, not to do cheap, manual labor.

• • •

Not too long after my conversation with Comrade Danasan, I went into the office of the municipal secretary, Mr. Ioan Ceanga. He invited me to sit down opposite him at his desk. Normally, this meant direct conversation.

All of a sudden he stood up and came around to stand next to me. He patted me on the shoulder and leaned down.

He said, "Muntean, do you know what your Christian brothers are calling you, the ones you are fighting for?"

I turned and looked up at him.

"No, I don't. Please tell me."

With his hand still on my shoulder, he said, "They say you're a traitor. They know you come to our offices daily and our work relationship has become a friendship. They believe you're betraying them. Instead of believing you are trying to resolve the problem, they think we are working together against them."

He walked back to the other side of his desk, sat down, and looked me straight in the eye. I had just learned what it felt like to be kicked in the stomach. Sadness settled on my heart. It was easy to see why some of the people had come to that conclusion.

I gathered my thoughts.

I said, "They're looking for a logical explanation because I'm the only one in the community working on their behalf. They've forgotten I borrowed money to help with the purchase of the property."

I took a deep breath and sighed.

"They're my brothers and can believe what they choose. I can't convince them differently. One day they'll know the truth, but from today forward I'm through. If I'm being called a traitor by the very community I've been trying to help, then I can no longer help them from this place."

I was surprised by my words. I do not know what Ceanga saw in my facial expression or read into my words, but his eyes widened.

He asked, "What do you have in mind?"

At that moment I made an irrevocable decision. I knew the answer to the intimidation and threats toward my children's futures.

"I'll leave this country, due to the threats made against me and my family, for our personal beliefs and my association with the Christian community."

The expression on his face as I left his office made me think he regretted saying what he had said. Whether or not it was the case mattered not—for me it was too late. The only thing left to do was to figure out how to make it happen.

Emigration from Romania was possible only if it benefited the Communist agenda and Ceausescu.

CHAPTER 12

ENEMIES

When a man's way are pleasing to the Lord, He makes even
his enemies to be at peace with him.
—Proverbs 16:7, NASB

THERE WAS NO TURNING BACK. Somehow, we were going to leave Romania.

But how?

On the way home from my meeting with Ceanga, I ran into my brother-in-law, Liviu. We spoke for a moment, and he asked me if there was anything new happening. I doubt he expected to hear what I was about to share with him. I told him about my conversation with Ceanga, and my decision to leave the country.

I continued, "Liviu, I live for my kids and want them to have the opportunity for their lives Stela and I never had. Also, I've done everything for our Christian brothers I can."

"John, I've been thinking about doing the same thing for some time, but didn't want to leave my parents behind. I need to talk to my father."

At that moment we saw his father Zaharia walking across the

railroad tracks carrying some wildflowers and medicinal herbs.

Liviu said, "Wait here, I want to go and talk to him right now and see what he thinks."

I watched as they stood and talked for a few moments, and then separated. Liviu came back with a big smile on his face.

"What did he say?"

"I told him what you were going to do and what I wanted to do, but explained my hesitation in leaving them behind. He told me if I wanted to go with you to America, I should go and not to worry about them. He would check to see if there was any way they could join us."

Excitement shone in Liviu's eyes. "Let's go right now and apply for passports."

"Before I do anything, I have to talk to Stela. Then, I need to go to the American Embassy to make certain we can get a visa to enter the U.S. Once I know we can then we'll go apply together for our passports."

Communist Party members had more freedom to travel abroad, as well as citizens who had sufficient reason to return to Romania. If the Romanian Communist Party (RCP) felt like a person was a flight risk, however, travel was forbidden.

I knew it was unwise to tip our hand. Besides, there was no point in applying if I could not get political asylum in the United States. Even getting into the American Embassy was a challenge.

• • •

True to form, Stela agreed, but with the clear understanding we were all to leave, not just me. One of her older brothers had escaped Romania while on a trip to Austria. Two and a half years passed before he, and his wife and children were reunited in Anaheim, California.

Although it was against the law to listen to Radio Free Europe, which was supported by the United States, Romanians with a radio listened. If a Romanian was caught listening to Radio Free Europe, the person went to prison.

The announcers often told stories of people attempting to connect with the Americans. We had heard the guards around the American Embassy were specially-trained Communist soldiers. Anyone attempting to enter the embassy was detained and questioned in a special holding room.

They did not tell us where, but if the answers were not to their liking, often the person(s) was beaten severely. Some never recovered.

In late October 1977, I drove alone to Bucharest and stayed overnight with some friends, but for their protection I did not tell them about my plans.

Earlier in the spring, Bucharest had been the epicenter of a devastating earthquake. Although the sidewalks and streets had been cleared of piles of residual brick and mortar, the damage to the buildings had not been touched.

I drove my car and parked it a couple blocks from the American Embassy. The grey building took up an entire block. It appeared to have survived the earthquake with no damage, despite its age.

Its French architecture was quite old and beautiful, and the structure was surrounded by wrought iron fencing. A well-manned guard station stood in front.

Blizzard-like conditions, with heavy snow blowing sideways, made me almost invisible to the group of Romanian soldiers who guarded the American Embassy. Several soldiers were at the front gate entrance, and more stood at the front corners. I braced myself and pushed into the wind as I surveyed the remainder of the area.

It was critical to not draw their attention. The long black wool coat and furry Russian ushanka not only kept my head warm, but helped me blend in with the others on the street who rushed to work or hurried toward the breadlines. From across the street I studied the backside of the embassy.

There has to be a way inside without being stopped.

As I skirted the building, I noticed many people dressed the same as me as they walked unhindered past the lone security guard at the back gate. They appeared to be employees.

With my briefcase in one hand, I flipped up my collar and pulled down the earflaps on my hat to hide my face. Only my eyes were visible. I quickly crossed the street pretending to be an employee. I went through the gate toward the back entrance.

Five feet from the threshold, the guard yelled, "Stop!"

I did not stop. I rushed through the back door.

Thankful to be inside and safe, I took a moment to look around. The room opened into a large reception area with chairs positioned around it for visitors. The back wall was lined with hooks filled with coats and hats. To my left, a young woman sat at a reception station enclosed with windows.

No one noticed me at first; I assume they thought I worked there. Finally, the young woman looked up, apparently surprised to see a non-employee.

"May I help you?"

I walked over.

"I'd like to see the ambassador to talk with him about my family and me. We hope to immigrate to the United States. I want to make certain we can have entry before applying with the government here."

"One moment please."

She turned and went into an office. After a few minutes she came out and asked me to follow her. I was taken into the office of Ambassador Harry G. Barnes, Jr. who had served as ambassador to Romania since March 1974.

The ambassador stood and offered me a seat opposite him at his desk. He had a quizzical look on his face.

He asked, "Mr. Muntean, how can I help you? First, however, tell me how did you get into the embassy?"

His smile, which tugged at the corners of his mouth, grew broader and never left his face the entire time I told him.

I filled him in about my meetings with Danasan and Ceanga, and the issues with my Christian community. I explained everything I had done over the past four years in an effort for the church to take possession of the property purchased in 1973.

I told him what my wife and I had experienced because we would not deny our faith. I explained I did not want my children persecuted for theirs.

"Why do you want to go to the United States?"

"Not for the money. I have that here. I want a future for my children. There's none here—under communism—because they're Christians, unless they deny their faith."

The ambassador continued to ask questions as he filled out paperwork. I do not know if it was the usual process, but he completed the paperwork from beginning to approval. I believe I was given political asylum at that time.

Finally finished, he put the paperwork in a file folder.

He said, "Mr. Muntean, this is your case file, dated with my approval. Everything that needs to be done from this end has been done. You're approved for an entry visa when you're ready to leave Romania. Unfortunately, we can't help you with your government."

Grateful for his help, I said, "I understand. This is my fight. I don't know how I'll get permission, but I will. Thank you very much."

We shook hands and I left his office. Then, I focused on how to get past the security guard in back.

When I put on my coat and hat, I did as before with my hat and collar, so only my eyes were visible. I stepped outside. From the distance, it looked like the guard had a camera in his hand, not a rifle. Head tucked against the wind, I walked fast and scratched my forehead to obscure my face.

The guard never attempted to stop me. Of course, that might have been because it would have been dangerous for him to let anyone know he had messed up.

• • •

Once safely home, I had no idea about the long journey, or danger which awaited my family. The Communist government of Nicolae and Elena Ceausescu did not take kindly to its citizens' desire to leave. It did not look good, and for the government, it was all about appearances.

An enormous lie had been woven in the free world about Romania's productivity, religious freedoms, and open-minded policies. Although its Constitution, Article 14 promised freedom of speech and religion, it was a farce. The West was led to believe its brand of communism was much different than that of the Soviet Union and China—Romania's deceit was successful.

$$\bullet \ \bullet \ \bullet$$

I returned home and began the process. My brother-in-law and I applied together for our passports. At the same time, I formally notified the Sighisoara municipality about my intentions. Inspector Tonco, the Ministry of Cults official, scheduled a meeting with the Pentecostal regional pastor, Gusty Berindeanu, and the president of the Pentecostal churches over Romania, Pavel Bochianu.

Tonco must have ordered these religious leaders to talk some sense into me. Pastor Gusty Belindeanu was sent to pick me up. I assumed they intended to change my mind about leaving Romania.

I listened respectfully to them, and then I laid out the entire history of constant delays. I also discussed the six written extensions and numerous verbal promises indicating the land was to be released to the church. I further told them about the meetings with Danasan and Ceanga, as well as the fact my Christian brothers had called me a traitor, and even accused me of stealing some of the church's money.

Pastor Pavel Bochianu was the first to respond.

"John, please be patient. I have a written promise with the necessary signatures. The church will receive the use permits within three months."

He held the paper out to me which I took and read. It was just like the others.

"I already have six of these in writing, so I don't believe a word of it. It's a lie."

"Brother Nelu, if it's a lie this time, then that means I'm lying with them."

I told him I accepted the terms of this request because of him, but I did not believe a word of it, or trust the others who signed it. However, if the permits were issued within the three months, I would renounce my petition to leave Romania.

• • •

One day before the three-month period expired, I went to see the municipal secretary for the Communist Party, Ioan Ceanga. His office provided oversight for Sighisoara and the surrounding smaller cities. His office was to issue the order to take possession of the property.

I said, "You know the time expires tomorrow for the use permits to be issued to the church."

He looked at me and shook his head.

"John, if I were to move the Lemeta Company out of the building, I wouldn't be in this office tomorrow. A higher power would have to do it."

Unsurprised, I told him of the meeting three months prior

and the promises made.

I then said, "From this point on, regardless of what happens with the church taking possession of the property, I'm done. I won't do another thing to help. My focus is to get my family out of Romania."

• • •

Liviu and I waited for passport approval. It did not come. Three months passed and the official deadline for approval had expired. I requested a meeting for a hearing at the passport office. The meeting was denied, and I was informed my passport would not be approved.

I insisted on a hearing with the commander of the secret police, General Hristea, whose function and authority included control over the municipal and regional secret police. The meeting took place in early 1978 in Targu Mures.

I waited in the outer office and listened to loud, angry voices echo down the hallway. A man rushed out of an office and appeared to be disoriented. The secretary called my name and took me through the same door the previous gentleman had exited. I opened it and went inside.

General Hristea, about 5'10"—an imposing, intimidating figure of a man with black hair—showed me where to sit. It was obvious he was still angry from the previous confrontation.

He snapped, "What do you want?"

I sat down and said, "General Hristea, I'm not in a hurry, I have plenty of time. Please take some time and calm down. I can hear very well."

At that, he sat down, pulled out a drawer, and took out a cigarette. He lit it, took a deep drag, relaxed, and leaned back in his chair.

"Now, we can talk."

The tension in the room diffused. Much more relaxed he leaned forward.

He asked, "Why do you want to go to America? There're too many people out of work. There's too much crime, and they even have homeless people."

"General, I live for my children, and I've been told they have no future in Romania because they're Christians. Religion is truly free in America. I even heard the American president puts his hand on the Bible when he takes the oath of office. It's not free here."

I explained all the other issues as well. He listened to what I had to say, and then informed me the case would be reviewed. I was to wait for the answer.

I waited and waited. No answer came. I let a few months pass, and then I began the telephone calls. Each time the secretary asked my name, and then put me on hold. Finally, when she came back, she explained they were too busy, backlogged, and had no time available for another meeting with General Hristea.

It seemed impossible to get pass the secretary until one day it occurred to me informers who needed to report might say something different. Such as: "I need to report."

I tried again. The secretary answered, and I told her I needed to report to Comrade Hristea. She put me right through without asking my name.

"Sir, this is John Muntean from Sighisoara. I'd like to meet with you to discuss the approval of my family's passports."

This became our routine over the next couple years—I made the call, pretend to be an informer, and got through to the general on the telephone. He always put me off for a couple weeks before we met, and then we talked while he tried to convince me not to leave.

Again, he said, "Mr. Muntean, I'm not the only one to approve your passport, many people are involved. You'll need to wait to hear back."

I visited his office no less than twenty times. There was no question the regional party leadership and higher officials were hoping I would give up.

The continual harassment of my children in the school system, especially the two older boys, wore on me. Besides the religious persecution, I did not like the fact the older students were used for field labor to dig up potatoes the first few weeks of the school year.

One day while I stood on the sidewalk in front of the police station having a chat with someone, the police chief called to me from an upper window.

"John, please come up to my office."

Naturally I responded and went inside. Captain Soare, a man a few years older than me with dark hair and an easy manner, met me halfway up the stairs. We stood talking together for over an hour as he tried to get me to change my mind.

"John, great things are going to be happening in Romania, we'll have lots of money."

"That may be true, but what good is money if you have nothing to buy? I'll be happy to hear about Romania's good fortune from outside the country."

He pressed on, and then finally accepted the fact I would not change my mind. He leaned close to me, and patted me on the shoulder.

He said, "John, if you stay on this course, you'll leave soon."

At that point, I realized why he met me on the stairs. There were no microphones or anyone around to overhear us.

• • •

I appreciated his encouragement. Even though he was one of the most powerful men in the city and a member of the Communist Party, I knew he was a Christian because of an incident that had happened years earlier when he helped our church with a serious problem.

• • •

One Thursday morning in 1972, without any warning, the owner of the building we rented for church services had removed all of the benches used for seating during our meetings. He put them out on the sidewalk and in the street. Our entire congregation had no meeting place.

What the owner had done was illegal. My father-in-law, the head pastor, contacted me immediately, and asked me what I thought ought to be done. In Sighisoara, there were no buildings available to rent, had there been, approval would have come from the office of the Spatiu Locativ. Either way, we were stuck.

Captain Soare had enjoyed the free services of my shop. He

often said, "John, if you need anything, please let me know."

The time had arrived.

After work, I went to his apartment. When I approached his door, I heard the radio turned up loud. I knocked, and he swung the door open. He greeted me with open arms, and invited me inside his home.

"Come in and see how I feed my soul."

The radio was tuned to Voice of America which was broadcasting "Vocea Evangheliei" from the United States. Pastor Pete Popovici preached from the Romanian Baptist Church in Los Angeles. To listen to this program, of course, was illegal.

I was amazed at his enthusiasm and openness as he told me how when he went to Cluj to take his exams, he would find a church and go into it. There he would kneel to pray for a half an hour until the unbearable burden was lifted from his shoulders. No one in Cluj knew him and—by not wearing his uniform—he was safe.

It was evident to me he trusted me to not reveal what he had just shared.

"Why have you come to see me, John?"

I told him of the church's difficulty and asked for his help. He thought for a few minutes.

He then said, "John, if I sent a police officer out now, and ordered the owner to put back the benches, I would be accused of helping Christians. I can't help you without you filing a report. Have a letter of complaint drawn up, you and the pastor sign it, then stamp it with the church stamp, and bring it to the police station in the morning.

"When you arrive, ask the secretary for the recorded number.

This will guarantee it crosses my desk. Then, I'll send out a sergeant with the order for the owner to replace the benches or be arrested—his choice."

I thanked him and did as he had instructed. That very afternoon, the benches were back in the building, and we held church service on Sunday. I am sure the report of that incident to his superiors read quite differently.

• • •

Captain Soare knew me and about my determination. He tried to dissuade me that afternoon in the stairway, but I was uplifted by his final words and pat on the back.

Weeks, months, and over two years had passed; I was no closer to getting passport approval than when I first applied. The government believed I would give up. They did not know my resolve.

No—quitting was not an option. I simply needed to figure out how I was going to force them into approving our passports.

One day Captain Toma, head of the secret police in Sighisoara, came to my shop with material for an order for special seat covers for another official's car. Again there was no compensation for the work. Like the other times, we stood and visited awhile; however, there was no discussion of my plans to leave Romania.

Just before he left, he said, "John, you'll never be allowed to leave Romania."

"Why?"

"We need your services. They're too valuable and no one around can do what your shop can do."

At that moment, the idea came. I knew how to force the government to approve my passport. I did not think, however, it was going to almost cost me my life.

CHAPTER 13

PERFECT PEACE

Thou wilt keep him in perfect peace whose mind is stayed on Thee; because he trusts in Thee.

—Isaiah 26:3, NASB

MY PLAN WAS DANGEROUS, AND secrecy was critical. Only one person to know about it at the time was my wife. We talked and prayed, and then put our complete trust in God. Without God's protection, I was going to die.

In order for my plan to work, I needed to connect with the free world over Radio Free Europe which we listened to every day. I had heard about the upcoming International World Conference on Security and Cooperation in Europe in Madrid, Spain, on November 11, 1980.

I knew Romanian representatives would be in attendance because they desired to renew their favored nation status. In order to accomplish that, they had to continue to deceive the world regarding their improved human rights policies.

Radio Free Europe was the only source of information about the free world available to Romanians. Many citizens like us

159

had two radios.

When we needed to listen, we turned the radio up loud and set it next to the black government-supplied, bugged telephone. We used the other radio to simultaneously listen to the forbidden station. If we had been caught, the punishment was prison.

Most Romanians who had electricity also had radios. Broadcasts into Romania began at five o'clock in the morning, and continued until twelve o'clock midnight each day. This was how Europe, including Romania's brave citizens, learned about the different cases of suffering and methods of torture used in prisons. It was news from the free world.

Radio Free Europe had informers within Romania who fed them information. Plus, those Romanians who escaped had their tales to tell.

The information regarding my plan had to be smuggled out. If I, or anyone involved in helping me were caught, we faced certain arrest. I would end up in prison.

A close family friend who worked at the Prestarea Cooperative in Sighisoara began dating a gentleman from Germany. He came often to see her. Since he drove a German car, he was followed everywhere he went—a common practice with any foreigner who visited Romania.

There were times the couple, wanting to avoid the harassment, called to ask me to drive them around, so they were able to enjoy each other's company without the secret police tailing them. Over the preceding months, we had developed a friendship built on trust.

I asked for their help.

One evening, about five weeks prior to the plan's implementation, I told them I had figured a way to force the government to approve my passport to leave the country. I did not reveal any significant details, but explained in order for it to be successful, the information needed to be smuggled out to Radio Free Europe, the International Red Cross, and the organization which headed up the human rights advocacy organization in Washington, D.C.

I made it clear if they were caught, there would be severe consequences: certain imprisonment for the young lady, and the loss of entrance into Romania for her boyfriend—possibly imprisonment for him as well. If I were discovered, imprisonment was the best case scenario.

To this day, as a married couple, they do not want their names revealed. They agreed to take the risk, and for their assistance my family and I are forever grateful—not only our family owes a great debt to this couple, but also every Romanian citizen who was able to legally emigrate from Romania between 1981 and 1990.

Unable to connect the next day due to the mandated driving schedule, I had time to prepare three separate envelopes with the details of my plan, and then addressed and sealed them. Two evenings later, I picked the couple up and we went for a drive into a forested area. We made certain no one had followed us when I handed them the envelopes.

It was some time before I knew how the envelopes were smuggled out. Since telephones were tapped and conversations were listened to or recorded, the couple had to devise a plan of communication in order for the young lady to know the information had been delivered safely to Radio Free Europe.

Once the gentleman arrived home in Germany, he called to tell her the flowers, although very delicate, had arrived safely, but they had not been delivered to the family's address, yet. He promised to try the next day.

When he connected with Radio Free Europe by telephone, he was verbally treated and talked to as though he was a spy. Two announcers had been murdered by Romanian agents. Radio Free Europe had moved its location. Naturally, its personnel were very cautious and challenged him.

Over the length of the call, he convinced the station the information he had was legitimate, and it was not only for Radio Free Europe, but also for the International Red Cross and the Human Rights Advocacy group in Washington, D.C. He was given their address and the envelope was delivered to Radio Free Europe by certified mail.

It was not until he received the signature card back that he called his girlfriend. He told her the flowers had been delivered safely, still beautiful and green, with no damage to them.

Once I knew for certain Radio Free Europe had my plan and the date of its implementation, I wrote eight identical certified letters. I mailed out seven.

I started with letters sent to Nicolae Ceausescu and the Parliament. I also sent one to General Hristea, head of the Securitate and Targu Mures municipal police. The rest were sent to Captain Danasan, Mayor Bolindut, Captain Soare, and Comrade Ceanga. Finally, I hand-delivered a letter to Commander Toma, head of the office of the Securitate in Sighisoara—I was not uncomfortable in his office because I had done repairs to the office furniture, and padded the doors for better sound proofing.

Toma welcomed me into his office. He pointed to a chair opposite his desk and I sat down.

"John, what brings you here today?"

I smiled and reached into my pocket. I handed him the envelope. He looked at me, perplexed, then opened it and began to read. I sat and waited.

His eyes brightened and a small grin soon filled his face. He began to look around—his eyes darted from corner-to-corner to indicate the office was bugged.

Pacepa's book *Red Horizons* mentions how all official offices were bugged, all the way up to Ceausescu's quarters. When Ceausescu didn't want to be listened to, he and Pacepa would walk through the rose garden.

Toma said, "John, you do know to attempt to smuggle any information out of the country is illegal and punishable with imprisonment, right?"

I answered, "Yes, I know."

I knew he said what he said for the benefit of those who listened, yet as a real warning to me. He was a friend.

At that, we stood and shook hands. The smile never left his face.

With about a week remaining, all the certified postal signatures came back. All was set. After I received them, not one official spoke to me about the letter or my plan. As an interesting side note: from that point forward, Romanian officials were required to open a certified letter and read it before signing for it.

• • •

We missed the first two broadcasts from Radio Free Europe that morning. Those Romanians who did listen heard the following announcement at 5:00 AM:

> November 10, 1980 – From the headquarters of Radio Free Europe. It is reported that today, John Muntean of Str. CluJului #5, Sighisoara, Romania, has begun a hunger strike to force the Communist government of Nicolae and Elena Ceausescu to approve the legal emigration of him and his family out of Romania.

The citizens were stunned and the nation was rocked. I knew people were shocked because up to that time, few Romanians legally emigrated out without support and pressure from the outside world.

The night before, we had sat around the dinner table together for the last time until the strike was over. Stela and I explained to the children what I was doing and why.

"Kids, this is the last time I'll eat with you until the hunger strike is over. I don't know how long it will go, but I don't want you to worry. God will take care of me. Your mother will make a clear broth, which I'll drink. Other than that, I'll have no food."

I continued, "You'll be staying home from school until it's over."

I let them know I was not going to quit: period. I told them their freedom and future was the most important thing to me, and I wanted them to have what neither their mother nor I ever had because we were Christians.

The fact was no matter how good they were in school, or how

talented, their education was to end at completion of seventh grade unless they denied their faith. I told them I did not want them to suffer anymore because they were Christians.

Five pairs of eyes were fixed on me—Stela's; my fifteen-year-old son, Ovidiu's; Liviu's and sweet Tabita's, twelve and ten respectively; and our youngest son, Danny's, age eight. I was not able to read their thoughts.

Stela and I reassured them I was going to be fine. We talked and prayed. We put our faith in God to bring success. I never doubted for a moment God's faithfulness to see us through to a good end.

It was not easy on my wife. I do not believe a serious decision is ever easy on the family. Mine was no exception.

The idea of a hunger strike had come to me only weeks before. I knew nothing about its rules. I just thought you did not eat food. I did know some people had used this method to force their government into an action. For me, it was the leading of the Holy Spirit.

Day One of the strike began as any other day, except I ate no breakfast. My three employees came to work as usual, and we all worked together. My children stayed home as Stela and I had decided. This was our way to protect them for many reasons, but mostly so the government could not use them to stop me.

That morning we had visitors: twice. Two hours apart. Two different groups came. Members of the Securitate called on us.

They refused to give us their names, and spent thirty minutes hammering me with questions and threatening me. Their agenda was to instill such fear I would quit. When the first group failed, they sent in another round to try to persuade me.

Not only that, but from the first day forward, we saw someone watch our house with binoculars. They isolated us. The Securitate disconnected our telephone and made their presence outside our home obvious, and warned people away—not that the townspeople needed the warning.

Sometime that first morning, we heard the report on Radio Free Europe. The children thought it fun to hear our names over the radio. Every hour on the hour, Radio Free Europe mentioned my name and the reason for the hunger strike.

Day Two was a duplicate of Day One, except a doctor and nurse came with the department head of Internal Medicine from the hospital. It was their job to check me over to make certain I was not eating. They tried in vain to convince me to go to the hospital.

"John, you need to be in the hospital. It'll be safer for you. You'll have a private room and good care."

"No way . . . we've heard the whispers of people being given shots to make them crazy for a time, and some never returning to normal."

Day Three, I was hungry and we had new visitors. Another tactic to gain a foothold, to make me quit. The school principal, one of the teachers, and a professor came to our door, and wanted to come inside, but Stela stepped out on the porch and denied them entry.

They insisted on talking to me. Again my wife refused. At that point, they began to pressure her into letting the children come to school.

"It isn't good for them to miss so many lessons. It would take the children's mind off the situation during the day."

For twenty minutes, the principal tried to change my wife's mind. He failed.

In our years together, through all our tough times, I had learned how much strength my wife had when it was needed. It was, indeed, needed at the time.

Stela made it clear the children would stay at home until the strike was over—there was no way we were going to let them out of our sight. She let the visitors know we did not trust them. Besides, she and the children were protesting with me. In spite of threats of possible punishment, she refused.

Other than party people, no one dared be seen coming to our home. The news was on everyone's lips. If anyone in our city had not heard the news report, or the whispers flying around our town, they either did not have a radio or a friend to tell them.

Eventually, the entire country knew what I was doing. Hope began to build across our land . . . *maybe, just maybe.*

One day rolled into the next. My hunger pangs increased. Every hour on the hour Radio Free Europe reported the progress of the hunger strike and my condition. How they knew, I had no idea, but somehow they did.

I continued to work side-by-side with my men, the first week. I ate no food, not one morsel. Stela did make a broth, which I drank. We were unaware—according to international law pertaining to hunger strikes—I could have eaten some bread.

Every day the secret police chanted their mantra.

"You're bringing shame to your country. Why are you doing this? It isn't going to work and you'll be punished for what you did."

Their last threat always made it clear they could simply take me out and kill me, and nobody would know or care. However, they were wrong. The world cared, and I knew it.

I smiled and crossed my wrists as if ready for handcuffs and said, "Go ahead boys, and you'll have to answer to the world about what you did to me."

It did not win me any points.

The first week, the hardest part was the hunger. After seven days, my digestive system shut down and the pangs went away. The second week, a certain amount of weakness caused me to be unable to work at the shop with my men. I did supervise them throughout the rest of the hunger strike, as I had prepared work ahead of time for them.

The doctors repeated their warnings. We repeated our answers.

Since anyone seen coming to our home was assumed to be a collaborator, my father-in-law or brother-in-law slipped in after dark, separately; never together. They talked and prayed with us. Their encouragement helped; their prayers even more.

I did not waver at all. There were only two choices. Succeed or die.

The World Conference began the day following the start of my hunger strike. At the conference, human rights within all participating countries were addressed. Romania, which had been awarded Most Favored Nation Status (MFNS) for trade purposes since 1975, was up for its annual review.

Nicolae Ceausescu had pursued a line of policy independent of Moscow, so he was very successful as he created the illusion of improved human rights. In reality, his government's policies were second only to the U.S.S.R.'s in human rights violations.

When the Romanian representative rose to give the report on

even more improvements, the delegate from the United States stood, and held a document in his hand.

"Sir, if what you're reporting is true, then tell us what John Muntean of Str. Clugului #5, Sighisoara, Romania, is doing now."

The Romanian representative did not respond.

The U.S. delegate said, "I'll tell you. John Muntean has begun a hunger strike to gain approval for him and his family to legally emigrate from Romania."

To the conference, this was a direct violation of a MFNS requirement which stated citizens had to be allowed to emigrate out of the country freely. Romania's renewal was under threat of being denied.

Radio Free Europe had people at the conference, so they reported this information in their broadcasts. That was Day Fourteen of my hunger strike, and Day Thirteen of the conference. The next day, no secret police came to threaten me, nor any other day.

When the two doctors and one nurse arrived to check me, the head of Internal Medicine told the other two to leave the room. We knew and respected each other because my shop supplied all the sheets, pillowcases, and scrubs for the hospital. Once the door closed, he turned to me letting out a big sigh.

"John, you have no idea how much work you have caused me."

"What do you mean? How did I make you work?"

"They forced me to do all kinds of research into the international laws regarding hunger strikes. I had to get books and read all day and night."

I smiled and said, "I didn't know there were any laws governing hunger strikes."

The doctor continued, "Not only that, I have to be in my office every morning at 4:00 AM to answer a call from the International Red Cross to give them an update on your condition."

He looked me in the eye and said, "If something happens to you, this country will be in serious trouble."

I had wondered how Radio Free Europe knew about my condition each day.

The doctor elaborated, "There was a man in Germany who went on a hunger strike for twenty-eight days, desiring freedom; it's the international record. If you go longer, it'll bring great shame to Romania."

I smiled and said, "Tell them I'll break the German's record."

At that, he returned my smile and shook my hand. I do not know if my response was reported to those in charge, but the following day I received my last visitor. He told me something I never expected.

Prestarea Cooperative, through which hundreds of shops, including mine, offered services, was government-owned and controlled. It had a large number of party attorneys. The senior attorney was sent to threaten me.

"John, I know you know why they sent me to you, but I don't care. I just want to tell you to be careful what you do because you're either going to open the door for thousands or close the door for everyone forever."

That was Day Sixteen.

• • •

From Day Seventeen to Day Twenty-Seven, the only people who came to our house were the doctors to check my condition, and Stela's father and brother late at night. My days were filled with reading, sleeping, and visiting with the children. In the evenings, we talked and prayed together. I lay on the bed and one of them massaged my legs with lotion. Also, we listened to Radio Free Europe and its updates.

Physically, the worst I suffered was an equilibrium issue toward the end of the strike. If Stela did not correct my direction when I walked, I tended to veer left into the wall. I felt no hunger—I could have continued for weeks.

On Day Twenty-Seven, at 1:00 PM, the telephone which had been silent for almost four weeks rang.

John, the day after hunger strike.

John and Stela, the day
after hunger strike ended.

John, day after
hunger strike ended.

John right after hunger strike,
lost 35lbs in 27 days.

CHAPTER 14

GOOD SUCCESS

This book of the law shall not depart from your mouth, but
you will meditate on it day and night so you may be careful to do
according to all that is written in it; for then you will make
your way prosperous, and then you will have good success.
—Joshua 1:8, NASB

1:00 PM

December 6, 1980

THERE'S ONLY ONE REASON THE telephone rang. The government had caved.

I picked it up. The caller identified himself as head of the passport office from Targu Mures.

"John, you haven't died and you won't stop your hunger strike. So, we decided to let you go. We're approving your passport."

I responded, "Very good."

He continued, "So, now you've got to stop what you're doing, and stop Radio Free Europe from talking about you."

I chuckled. "I have nothing to do with Radio Free Europe.

I can't stop them, but maybe when you give me the documents, they'll find out about it the same way they've found out about everything else. Or, you can tell them to stop."

"Tomorrow, you need to come to the office in Targu Mures to get the papers."

Too weak to go anywhere, I answered, "My wife can come. That's too far for me to travel."

"That's fine, have her come tomorrow morning."

"Before we hang up there's one thing I want to make clear. You know there's a law that states once the documents are registered in your office, you have fourteen days to respond yes or no. If you don't give me an answer, I'll begin a second hunger strike. You can let Radio Free Europe know that, too."

"Just tell your wife to come get the paperwork."

My wife knew immediately what the call was about. Together, we rejoiced and thanked God for His faithfulness. The children were outside playing in the snow, sledding down the hill by our home. When they came in and we told them what happened, they were so happy—happy Daddy got to eat with them, and happy to see my beard go away.

What amazed us was the report two hours later at 3:00 PM from Radio Free Europe which declared the Romanian government had granted approval, and the hunger strike was over. My threat about a second hunger strike was also reported.

When the hunger strike had begun, neither Stela nor I knew anything about the proper way to begin or end a strike. Had I sat down to eat any solid food, especially a large portion, it may have cost me my life.

We credit God for the wisdom about what to do. Stela prepared a thick soup, with no chunks of food. I ate a small amount every two hours to begin to wake up my system.

In twenty-seven days I had lost thirty-five pounds.

I had been a bit overweight for my 5'8" height, so my weight loss was not considered a bad thing. However, I do not recommend doing it that way.

The next morning my wife and Liviu went to the passport office in Targu Mures. Liviu only intended to keep her company, but he was awarded the documents for his family at that time as well.

I may have won, but the government was not going to make it easy. There were hoops we still needed to jump through. Encouraged by my actions at the time I applied for our passports, other members of my wife's family had also applied. All of them were granted approval after my hunger strike.

A few days later, I felt strong enough to go into the city to begin the process of meeting the government's mandates. Everywhere I went, people greeted me, looked around to make certain they were not being watched, and then give me the thumbs up sign close to their chests.

Over the next week, I completed the required paperwork. I thought I had satisfied the government's requirements, such as providing proof from the cooperative which stated I had no debt. Due to God's amazing financial blessing on our lives, we had already cleared the mortgage debt years before.

I thought everything had been completed, so I was surprised to find out we could not leave the country if we owned a property.

The government was going to buy it from us, but they had to have it appraised.

Without hesitation, I said, "I'll do it. Just send an appraiser."

The lawful payout amounts at that time ranged from 5,000 lei to 80,000 lei which was to be paid to the owner. It did not matter whether the house was a shack or an apartment complex. No matter how large or well-equipped, the maximum compensation was 80,000 lei.

I was also informed I, along with my wife and oldest son, had to pay 1,200 lei each to leave the country and renounce our Romanian citizenship. The three younger children were exempt. Most citizens did not even earn 1,200 lei in a month.

God had already provided for us financially; therefore, it did not present us with a hardship. However, they dragged out a process which normally took an afternoon to complete to over weeks.

Weeks passed, and no appraiser came from Targu Mures, just fifty miles away. I repeatedly called, and was stalled by continual excuses. One day I drove to the office which handled appraisals and asked to whom I needed to speak. I went to the appraiser and told him my story and asked him why he did not come.

"They won't give me a car to drive there. I have my own car, but don't drive it in the winter. It's too dangerous."

I said, "If I come and get you, will you come?"

"Yes, I'll come."

It was the end of the day, and he was preparing to leave.

I asked, "Would you like me to give you a ride home? It's pretty cold and slippery out there."

"Sure, if you want to."

We walked out of the office to my car.

When we slid in the seats, he asked, "Where did you get these seats? Who made them for you?"

The Romanian car, the Dacia, came only with vinyl seats. At -30°, the seats felt like blocks of ice.

"Wow, I'd like to have something like these."

"If you come to appraise my house, I'll make you some."

"I'll come. Just let me know what day you want to pick me up."

"You tell me, and I'll have everything made for your car."

We agreed on a date. When I drove to Targu Mures to pick him up, I presented him with his new foam padded upholstered seat covers. I installed them for him.

It was illegal for the appraiser to share the real figures with the homeowner, but this gentleman, appreciative of my gift of foam-covered seat covers, showed me the real value of our house. Up to that point, we had no idea and there had been no way to find out.

After the second flood in 1974, we had added on the shop for the business, put in plumbing, and added a furnace in our basement for heat. Before then, our only heat source had been the wood stove Stela cooked on. When the appraiser told us the amount, we were stunned. He appraised it for 240,000 lei.

That same day he not only appraised my house, but also my father-in-law's and two brothers-in-law's homes. We were each given 80,000 lei. We could not say or do anything, but accept it.

On February 11, with everything completed, I drove to Targu Mures to the passport office to submit all the paperwork. From the point of registration, the clock began to tick. By law, I was to receive my answer in fourteen days on February 24, 1981.

Life continued as normal as possible. I worked in the shop with the employees. Stela worked with the ladies who made the sheets, pillowcases, and hospital scrubs. The children returned to their classes. Yet, day after day, there was no word.

On February 23, I called the passport office and was informed our passports were not ready because they were too busy. The office begged the question: how could I expect it to be done so quickly?

I responded, "All right. I told you if I hadn't received the answer by this time, I'd begin a second hunger strike."

• • •

On February 24, 1981, I began the second hunger strike, and prepared to continue as long as needed. How Radio Free Europe heard about it, I had no idea, but during its opening broadcast into Romania they announced it.

As before, the telephone rang at 1:00 PM.

"Come get your passports."

When I arrived at the passport office and looked at them, the actual date of approval was stamped February 17, seven days earlier. By 3:00 PM the same afternoon, Radio Free Europe reported I had the passports.

The passport not only had the approval date, but it also had the date set for us to leave Romania. We had three months to the day to arrange everything. On May 17, 1981, we were scheduled to board an airplane to freedom.

• • •

With so much to be done, we appreciated having three months to prepare. Each of us was allowed fifty pounds per suitcase. After sixteen years of marriage, four children, a home, and a business, how can we choose the most necessary fifty pounds? It is impossible. We had to walk away from it all. The price for freedom is never cheap or easy.

Once I received the money for the house—a couple weeks before our departure—I drove to the special office in Bucharest, the only place international tickets were purchased. We needed six tickets. I had already learned the total cost was 87,000 lei. Divided by six, it totaled one year's wages for each of us at 1,200 lei a month. Like I stated, they did not make it easy to leave.

Yet, again, God had already met our needs. At the airport office, I handed the young lady at the table all the documents for six tickets, and laid the Romanian lei on the table.

She said, "You can't buy tickets with Romanian lei. You have to have American dollars."

I took a couple steps back from the table and raised my voice.

"Ma'am, how could you ask me for American dollars, since I would be put in jail for even having one American dollar? I work in this country for Romanian money, not American."

"I'm sorry sir, but you can't buy tickets with Romanian money. Whoever called you to go to the states should've purchased your tickets?"

"Nobody called me to go the states. I wanted to go. I'm buying these tickets myself."

By that time everyone had gathered around me to see what was going on. The young lady stood up, took all my documents, and ran down the hall behind her into an office.

I stood there for about five minutes or so when the door opened. A very tall gentleman stepped out, looked at me, and put his forefinger to his lips, and then walked up to the table.

Quietly, he said, "We'll take the Romanian money."

I purchased six tickets to take us from Bucharest to Los Angeles, California. We expected to stay in Rome for a night or two, and then fly from Rome to New York City, then onto Los Angeles where we were to meet my wife's older brother.

• • •

Our last few weeks in Romania were bittersweet. From the first moment I had decided to walk the road on which we were traveling, I had asked my seventy-nine-year-old mother to join us. Never had we considered leaving her behind.

She said, "John, if your two sisters weren't here with me, I'd throw my arms around your neck and you would have to take me."

I remember her standing on her porch as she waved to us. She wiped tears from her face with her hankie. It was the last time I saw my mother. She passed away one year later.

• • •

What does one do with sixteen years of accumulated possessions in a Communist country? Give it away—everything. Find people who will be able to put it to use, they are everywhere.

If a person is not allowed to ship one single item—furniture, bedding, silverware, clothing, pots and pans, and dishes—only the hope for a bright new future softens the pain of which photograph to keep or toss into the fire. Only hope eases the sorrow and helps to throw treasured childhood memories into the flames.

Danny's eyes filled with tears as he realized his treasured braids had to be burned. Since Danny was the last of our children, Stela had not been able to bring herself to cut his hair until he was three. He had worn his hair in braids, and she had saved them.

"Mama, are you sure?"

"Yes, Danny. I'm so sorry, honey."

Our daughter, Tabita, had two dolls, Nicolet and Minerva. One doll was three-feet tall and the other was one-foot tall. Nicolet, with hair the color of Tabita's, had been a gift from me. She was Tabita's favorite. Minerva, the three-foot doll, was bald. Tabita loved her dolls and cried when they were given away. I felt her sadness along with her.

Furniture, bedding, pots, and pans are replaceable, but these items were not. Many tears were shed.

Nineteen other family members were preparing to leave at the same time we were. Friends from all over Romania came to say goodbye. Long into the night we talked, ate, visited, and gave things away. There was laughter, tears, congratulations, and well wishes.

Everyone within our large families and church family celebrated with us. We got maybe two to three hours of sleep each night. Our emotions ran high. Yet, in spite of tears, we were filled with hope and joy.

Not too long before we left, I was summoned to the office of the Securitate in Targu Mures—Captain Hristea had something he wanted me to understand. He made it clear we were not to speak of anything negative about Romania. We were to keep our mouths shut.

He said, "We'll see to it your Christian brothers get to take possession of the church property."

I guess he hoped that piece of information was going to encourage me to not talk about them.

I sat and listened quietly, and did not respond. When he was done and indicated it was time to go, he gave me one last warning.

"John, remember what I've said, because our long arm can reach all the way to America."

I nodded.

Could their arm truly stretch that great a distance?

• • •

The day before we were to fly out, we drove to Bucharest in our friend's car. Steve and Anna Poponut were gracious enough to loan us their car since the undercarriage of mine had rusted out from all of the salting of the roads. They flew down from Targu Mures, met us at the hotel to say goodbye, and drove their car back. It was good to be blessed with friends who helped us—most were not able.

We stayed in the hotel, all twenty-five family members flying out, plus many friends. We stayed up most of the night. The kids rode up and down the elevators. There was much to celebrate.

The next day at the airport, after we checked our bags, my father-in-law's suitcase was thrown so hard onto the conveyor belt, the zipper split. Most of his clothes spilled out. There was a great deal of confusion, and airport personnel refused to let him gather his clothes.

I told them I had the tools in my bag to sew the zipper closed, but needed to get them from my bag. They allowed me to do it.

What they did not know was I had a large sum of Romanian lei in my inside jacket pocket. It was illegal for us to take Romanian lei out of the country, but I had needed it to pay the cost of the hotel and food. As far as the government was concerned, they had no problem if you left penniless.

More dangerous than having Romania money, I had made arrangements to trade lei with an American tourist for dollars. I had carefully sewn nearly two hundred dollars into the shoulder pads of my jacket. It was easy to match the stitches when I closed the seam on the pads.

When I got my tools and thread from my bag, I slipped my hand into the inside of my jacket and grabbed a handful of Romanian lei. I hid it in my bag. The rest of the lei I gave to our friends. By the next time the Securitate conducted their last search of everyone, I had already passed it on.

We said our goodbyes and boarded the airplane. There were business people on the airplane, possibly tourists who had visited Romania. To my knowledge we were the only emigrants. We were scattered throughout—couples and families seated quietly. There was little talking. Young and old were headed to a new life.

Only Stela's parents, who were on the airplane with us, had known what it was to truly live free. They had already been adults when the Nazis first arrived, followed so closely by the Soviets. They remembered tables full of food, freedom to come and go, and the opportunity to move wherever you chose. Stela's brother, Liviu, was a small boy like me when the Communists took control of the country, so we had experienced a small taste of freedom.

The rest of the families on board had only lived under the reign of terror, the constant knowledge at any moment, a mother, father, brother, or sister may be taken by the Securitate, never to be seen again. They had waited in breadlines, only to be turned away because the shelves were empty. They had suffered as pocaits.

I sat and waited. I knew at any moment the pilot could be ordered to turn the airplane around to take us back. All the way to Italy, I did not relax because I knew how the government operated.

Soon, though, we began our descent. The ground came up to meet us—the airplane, touched down. The brakes screamed as they slowed the airplane on the tarmac. Finally, the jet came to a stop.

I released a sigh of relief, smiled, and gratefully whispered: "Freedom!"

Ovidiu.

Liviu.

Tabita.

Danny.

1978 (back row, left to right) Liviu, Stela, John, Ovidiu.
Tabita and Danny (front row).

Funeral procession in Romania for John's mother "Anica."
Anica died one year after John came to America.

CHAPTER 15

TAPESTRY

We know that God causes all things to work together for good
to those who love God and are called according to His purpose.
—Romans 8:28, NASB

WHAT DOES FREEDOM FEEL LIKE? Does it have a smell?

According to our oldest son, Ovidiu, it smelled like heaven. He said Rome had a sweet fragrance that filled the air. Everything was clean and bright. All around people laughed and sang. They walked about without checking over their shoulders. They spoke freely. No one seemed concerned they might be monitored.

When we had gotten off the airplane, we saw a gentleman hold a sign with our name on it: Muntean. He spoke a little Romanian and welcomed us, and then beckoned for us to follow him to the bus which took us to an apartment complex for emigrants awaiting documents to be processed. We were all supposed to have sufficient accommodations and food provided.

The six of us had two twin beds in a small room and thin pads which covered a net. We tried to manage two people per bed, but the sagging middle prevented it. Our four children slept on the floor.

Breakfast, lunch, and dinner consisted of spaghetti with French rolls. Once, Liviu did not want the sauce and asked for noodles without it. No problem. Evidently, the cook had no problem washing off the noodles. When the plate came back no sauce was visible until a noodle was picked up, and wet, runny sauce ran from the center of the plate.

We met several others in the building and were quite surprised when they told us how long they had been there—anywhere from six months to almost two years. They said the country they were going to was not ready for them.

I did not know the exact date we were to fly out, but I did know our entry into the United States had been approved almost four years earlier. They were ready for us, and we for them.

The children's excitement reminded me of Christmas mornings. Their eyes were bright with anticipation, and they were eager to find out what awaited us out there. Stela and I laughed. It did our hearts good to see their joy.

Liviu remembers watching from a window as four men picked up a double-parked Fiat, and moved it onto the sidewalk, so a delivery truck was able to pass by. He also remembers the joy of making some money for his hard work; so different from being made to help bring in the harvest with other students. He and a couple friends helped unload a truck full of bread and glass drink bottles.

All three sons—Ovidiu, Liviu, and Danny—along with other boys from the compound, ran and played for three days.

We decided to take advantage of the free time to do some

sightseeing. We spent a great deal of money on the kids, though probably not much by American standards. We rode the busses around to various sites. The Roman Coliseum was amazing, the sights and sounds of life-as-usual surrounded us. Six pairs of eyes stared in awe.

Markets filled with foods, produce, and all kinds of baked goods kept us shaking our heads. We had never seen such abundance. The memory that sticks with me was going out the front door of the complex when I saw a meat market a few doors down.

I looked at the half pig and quarter beef hanging in the window. It looked so perfect I assumed it must be plastic. I went inside to get a good look. Another man walked pass me and asked the butcher for the half pig in the window. I could not believe my eyes when I saw the butcher take it down. It was real.

I said to myself, *Wow, this is freedom.*

In the evenings, people sat outside at restaurants, and talked and laughed into the night. Laughter was heard everywhere. That was not a sound common on the streets of Sighisoara.

Even though we enjoyed Rome, we knew all of us could not continue to share those two tiny beds. The other Romanian families were similarly crowded. My brother-in-law and I went to the American Embassy and spoke with the ambassador.

We let him know we were aware money had come from our supporters from the States to pay for two persons to a room, like a hotel. It was obvious something was not right, and we were not going to accept it.

I do not know what the ambassador thought, but he did not appear happy.

He responded, "Be ready at 5:00 AM. You'll be leaving for the States."

That was fine with us. When the word got out to others who stayed in the same building, they came to us with questions such as: how could we be leaving after only four days? We had no answers for them, but were grateful to be on our way.

The next morning all twenty-five of us flew out of Rome on PanAm Flight #747. The children were delighted with the coloring books and Captain's wings pinned on their shirts. We enjoyed our airplane food.

We flew into John F. Kennedy International Airport in the early evening, and actually saw the Statue of Liberty. We had no idea of its significance. We just wondered how it was built in the water.

After landing, and in order to make our connecting flights, our families separated as we went through customs. When Stela, the kids, and I started through, I handed the young customs officer my passport. She examined it, looked at me, and then checked information on a screen.

"Please wait here."

She left and was gone for several minutes. When she returned she had a green card in her hand which she handed me.

I looked at both sides and asked, "What do I do with this?"

"This is your identification card. Do not lose it. Keep it on you for the rest of your life. Your family will get theirs in about six months."

I did not understand why I had received my green card and the others had not. To this day, I assume it was because I was given political asylum. There were no further delays before we boarded our airplane to Los Angeles.

• • •

We were blessed to have Olympiu, Stela's brother, in the Los Angeles area to prepare for our arrival. He was well-established in a tight-knit Romanian community.

When it was our turn to settle in America, he found an apartment for us, purchased some beds and living room furniture, and filled the refrigerator with food. Fortunately, I had been able to send enough money to the United States to facilitate the purchases. We were about to begin our new life.

Within the first couple of days we made a trip to the supermarket. We walked the aisles in awe of the stocked shelves. By the time we left, our basket almost overflowed with food. With no car, we had to walk.

The adjoining clothing store caught Stela's attention. She wanted to see what they had to offer.

I thought: *We can't take the basket in the store . . . but this is America. No one will steal it.*

When we came out, it was gone. My heart sank. I had been wrong about my new country. We walked home to get more money and returned to the supermarket. No sooner had we walked in than the manager came up to us.

"Someone saw your basket of groceries and brought it in, so it wouldn't get stolen," he told us.

So, I had been right!

We were shocked, however, to learn some people in America

choose to tease and show acceptance by egging a house or toilet-papering the trees. Evidently, we were well-liked.

Ovie caught one of the boys, so we called the police. After the officer spoke with the young man, he explained it was because they liked us. A family in the complex confirmed it. We accepted what he said, and asked for it to be shown differently. In Romania, eggs were precious and no one wasted toilet paper which was not even available on a regular basis until around 1955.

Being Pentecostal, we did not have a television. So, although the children saw a few shows at their friends' homes, nothing prepared us for America's abundance and modernization.

The freeways were crazy, skyscrapers were huge, and super-markets were packed with food on every shelf—rows of cheeses, salamis, and so many different kinds of lunch meats. At first, when we walked the aisles of the stores, we were afraid to touch anything. Shops of every kind, businesses, and restaurants were everywhere. Oh, and Disneyland.

We only learned our apartment had air-conditioning after we spent several very hot nights sleeping on the floor next to the windows, or out on the concrete patio. Stela's brother came to check on us.

I said, "Everything is good, but it's so hot we can't sleep in our beds."

Olympiu burst out laughing.

"Why don't you turn on your air-conditioning?"

That night we slept in our beds.

Back in Romania, people had smuggled in American maga-zines, and sometimes tourists left them. Still, one had no idea; it was exciting and scary.

Within two weeks, Stela and I enrolled in English class. We attended every night, five days a week, for one and a half years. The children had already begun to learn English in Romania. I paid an American-Romanian lady, whose family had returned to Romania prior to the Communist takeover, to teach them.

Determined for the family to learn English in America, I did not allow Romanian to be spoken in the house for three years. Danny almost forgot the Romanian language entirely.

The very first Sunday, we attended the Romanian Church of Melodyland. The pastor was Dr. Emmanuel Deligiannis. The church body, numbering sixteen until twenty-five of us joined, rented a large sports room at the school attached to the Melodyland Church in Anaheim. We were making headway.

Later in the week, we went to the immigration office to register. We were directed to the social security office. There it was made clear: until we learned some English, I should not try to get a job.

Going without work was strange and uncomfortable to me. The social security people gave me the address of an office which supplied financial help. We counted it a blessing to have the United States government help us in our new homeland. Yet, I intended to use it only as long as absolutely necessary.

Within nine months, I had learned enough English to get a job in an upholstery shop for cars and boats. It was a blessing because I learned about the kind of sewing machine used in the States and the tools needed for this type of service. The tools were very different from the ones I had used in Romania. Although the pay was minimal, what I learned was extremely important.

Not long after, we made friends with an Assembly of God pastor who was pleased to learn I was skilled in reupholstering as well as carpentry. He wanted to pay me for the carpentry jobs and repair work to some of the furniture I had done for him, and would be doing.

I explained since it could not be full-time work, I still needed the government assistance. By this time I knew I was a full-fledged Capitalist.

I wanted my own business and had already shared my dream with him. The pastor's solution for paying me for ongoing side work was to purchase the needed tools in order for me to open my upholstery shop. I stored it all in my garage.

In the winter of 1982, work at the car/boat upholstery shop slowed down. As the last one hired, I was the first to be laid off. Not too long afterwards, a mechanic I knew told me he could not find a convertible top for his Alpha Romero and wanted to know if I could do a top. I did. When he came to pick up his car and saw it, he was amazed.

"John, why don't you open your own shop? You do amazing work."

I answered, "I would, but you need money to open up a business."

"I have an extra stall I can give up, and it's only three hundred dollars a month. I'll talk to the landlord about your using it."

When people talk about the need for huge sums of money to begin a business, I smile. When the mechanic came back to me, he had worked it out, with only the first month required—I was in business. I had one hundred dollars in my pocket, and I borrowed the remainder.

In February 1983, I applied for a business license. The license was dated March 1, 1983. We were in this country less than two years before I had my own business.

I went to the welfare office and told its personnel what I was doing.

I explained to the lady at the counter, "I'm starting a new business and don't know what to do. When I make money and report it to you, the assistance will be cut and I won't be able to run the business and still support my family. "

She looked at me and said, "Mr. Muntean, in the twenty years I've worked here, no one has ever come to me with that question. I don't know the answer, but will get my supervisor."

She left and another lady came to the counter. I explained my situation again.

"Mr. Muntean, I have worked here for twenty-five years and never had anyone come tell me they wanted to start a business. Let me get my supervisor."

I continued to wait. Finally, a tall blond lady came toward me with a big smile.

She said, "You're the kind of people we need."

Before she continued, I interrupted her.

"Let me tell you what I want to do."

She said, "I already know. This is what I suggest you do. With all your profits from the business, you should purchase any needed tools and materials required to do the work. At the end of the month, bring us all your receipts. If you have a one hundred dollar profit, we'll cut your aid that amount. Try to use all the money you make toward business needs if you can."

I reported to the welfare office each month. Finally, after nine months, I walked into the office with a thank you letter. I told them I did not need any more help. It made me feel good to be on my own.

No doubt, God had richly blessed our lives. I owned my own business, the kids were doing well in school, and we had a wonderful growing church community. In the two years we had attended, it grew from sixteen people to over one hundred sixty.

Sometimes, Ovie used his musical talent to play the piano during worship. On Sunday July 17, 1983, after the evening service, Dr. Deligiannis asked me if I would come to his home the next evening to discuss a matter.

Once we got past the pleasantries, he asked, "Why don't the Romanians here give enough money to support the church?"

I answered, "In our church in Romania, once the offering was collected, we had two men count it and make two reports—one for me and one for them. Once the service was over, the money was brought to me."

In the two years we had attended this Romanian Church in America, I had noticed the two men who collected the offering take it to the pastor, who then took it home. I had never said a word about the process, but when he asked me, I did not shy away from the truth.

"Pastor, we also had a church meeting once a year to share with the members how much money had been received, how it had been spent, and what was left. You haven't done any of this. The people only see the offering taken, and then the money going into your hands. Until they're comfortable with what is happening with the money, they won't give much."

Another one of the reasons for concern among congregants was the selection of the two gentlemen who regularly collected the money. One, a very nice man, appeared to be somewhat mentally disabled. At least, enough so when he was given a ride home, he could not point out his house or give his address.

The other gentleman had some physical disabilities. Neither man seemed to understand the way they physically touched the pastor after giving him the offering was inappropriate in front of the church. The way they laughed and patted his stomach was very odd.

I addressed this fact with the pastor and suggested he stop the men's behavior because the young people made fun of him and the other two men. He thanked me and suggested we pray together, which we did.

Two days later on Wednesday, I received a certified letter informing me that my family and I were excommunicated from the church. No reason was given for this action. We were ordered to never return. If we did, Dr. Deligiannis threatened to call the police. The letter was dated July 18, the same day as our meeting.

Besides his signature, there were seven others. One signature was from the man who collected the offering and was unable to find his house; two signatures were from his sisters; and one signature was from his brother-in-law, and three other people—all related to him in some way.

The letter went on to say this was legally binding. Not only were we excommunicated, but so were Liviu, Stela's brother, and his family. Liviu and I were closer than many biological brothers.

Being uneducated in such matters and how they are handled in

FREEDOM TO THE CAPTIVES INTERNATIONAL MINISTRIES
Rev. Emmanuel A. D. Deligiannis, Ph.D., General Superintendent

Incorporated as:
The General Conference of the Romanian
Pentecostal Churches of North America

P.O. Box 6366
Orange, California 92667

The Spirit of the Lord is upon me; because the Lord hath anointed me to preach good tidings unto the meek. He hath sent me to bind up the brokenhearted, to proclaim liberty to the captives and recovering of sight to the blind, to set at liberty them that are bruised, to preach the acceptable year of the Lord. (Luke 4.18-19)

July 18, 1983

Dear Mr. Muntean:

We the presbyters hereby notify you that you are excommunicated from the Romanian Church of Melodyland. According to the rules, you are thus prohibited from attending our services. We hope you understand that this decission is legally binding. We also hope that you understand the severity of your condition. Please know that this includes your son Ovidiu and your entire family.

Noi Presbiterii va notificam ca sunteti excomunicati (exclusi) din Biserica Romana Melodyland. Conform regulelor vi se interzice sa mai q atendati servicurile noastre. Speram ca intalegeti ca aceasta decizie este legala si finala. Deasemeni speram ca va dati seama de severitatea cazului Dstra.

Sincerely,
THE PASTORS

Dr. Emmanuel Deligiannis

Dr. Theophilos Deligiannis

Dr. Daniel Bieber

EADD: jm

Church Secretary
Mary V. Von Berg
Mary Von Berg

Corporation Secretary
Elisabeth Pascu
Elisabeth Pascu

Sunday School Superintendent
Jeffrey MacSwan

Church Program Director
Dr. Petru Oanca

John and Stella Muntean and Family
2147 Oertley Dr.
Anaheim, Ca. 92804

P 428 651 529

the United States, I did not know what to do. I contacted the head of the Melodyland Church and informed him of everything that had happened.

He told me he and I would go to the Thursday night service. He wanted to observe. So, he and I, along with my son, Ovie, went that evening.

The end of the evening saw my son, Ovie, being released from the back of a police car. The majority of the congregation was shocked when the pastor called the police and had my son arrested while he sat quietly in the back row of the church. They chose to no longer sit under his leadership. His church attendees dwindled to a scattered few.

In order to protect his reputation and justify his actions, he began to spread lies about me and threatened to have us deported. Not knowing if he had that kind of power, I sent a letter to the U.S. Immigration department.

One day I received a call in answer to my letter. It was from the department's head office in Texas, wanting to know how they could help. We discussed what had happened. The person on the other end of the line assured me no one could have me deported. He told me to stay away from the pastor's family—they could not do anything. They just tried to scare me.

He said, "John, we know all about your struggle in Romania, the things you suffered, and what you did to come to this country. You don't need to worry about getting deported."

He then asked, "Did you know Deligiannis is an informer for the Securitate in Romania?"

Shocked, I said, "No way. How could a pastor be an informer

and report on his Christian brothers? If he is, then why don't you arrest him?"

"John, we have the proof; however, our witnesses are in Romania. The government is not going to let them come testify. Just stay away from his family. Again, don't worry, he can't do anything to get you deported."

How many more informers were out there?

CHAPTER 16

AMBUSH

Deliver me from mine enemies, O My God and set me
securely on high away from those who rise up against me.
For behold they have set an ambush for my life . . .
—Psalm 59:1, 3, NASB

ONE WOULD THINK SINCE I had lived in another country for seven years, the interest of the secret police in me had ceased. After the incident in 1983 with Pastor Deligiannis, I did not give his threats much thought.

God's financial blessings, once again, poured on us as a result of my wife's and my blessing a Romanian Pentecostal Church in Targu Mures which had been demolished by the government with bulldozers. We ordered a new organ and all the sound equipment from a factory in Italy in 1984, and donated it to the church.

In 1985, we purchased a nice home in Costa Mesa, where my business was located. The kids were doing well in school. Our children were fortunate enough to attend the Melodyland Christian School because I did repair work for the school on the side.

We were quite happy in our new church, The Upper Room,

with Pastor Floyd H. Lawhon. What an amazing man.

I need to take a moment to share how heartbroken I was when my family was ex-communicated and kicked out of the Romanian Church. To learn the pastor was an informer was unbelievable.

I had sat under his leadership for two years. My attempt to find another Romanian church failed. I was tired of preachers who tried to control their congregation. I had certainly witnessed this in Romania; I wanted no part of it in America.

One evening while my daughter, Tabita, was at choir practice for another church, I walked across the complex into the Upper Room Church, in Westminister. It was filled with people singing, raising their hands in praise, and praying. Laughter and joy filled the room.

The presence of the Lord washed over me as I walked in. After being greeted with wide smiles and hand-shakes, I was asked if I needed prayer.

"Yes!"

I learned then God is still in the heart-mending business, and I had found my spiritual home.

Pastor Lawhon and his wife became close personal friends. They still are today, though they live in Louisiana.

On September 22, 1987, a proud day for the Muntean family, Stela stood with three thousand immigrants with raised right hands who swore their allegiance to the flag and America. My heart swelled with pride and joy. I raised my hand in solemn pride only two months later on November 17, 1987.

We were officially American citizens. Lee Greenwood's song "Proud to be an American" is a favorite of ours.

In the fall of 1988, Pastor Lawhon and his wife decided to take a trip with Stela and me, as we traveled through several European countries. Romania was to be our last stop. Pastor Lawhon, one of the nineteen leaders of the International Church of God, wanted to visit several of the Pentecostal churches across Romania.

We planned to be there for two weeks. I translated for him when he was asked to speak.

The trip was our first time back in Romania. Most of our relatives, sixty-nine to be exact, had already immigrated to America within the first two years of our emigrating out of Romania. We looked forward to seeing the rest of our family members and spending time with our friends.

After we spent time in Germany, we enjoyed some time in Austria, and then went on to Italy. From Italy, we traveled through Yugoslavia to Romania where we attempted to enter the country at the large border crossing. We arrived at 1:00 AM in an older model Mercedes with different-colored doors, trunk lid, and fenders. The German head of the Church of God had lent it to us, hoping its appearance limited suspicion.

The Yugoslavian border guards checked our passports and waved us through. The Romanian border guards were waiting for us.

Informers in America had reported to the Securitate about our anticipated trip. The guards knew we were coming, and it was their job to find some reason to prevent us from entering.

Five guards—four men and one woman—took everything out of the Mercedes during their search. They completely emptied the suitcases and examined every piece of clothing, even our rolled up dirty laundry.

I said to the female guard, whose job it was unroll and inspect each piece, "You must love that job, right?"

She ignored me and stayed focused on what she was doing.

My wife, Stela, knowing a female guard might be at the border crossing, had prepared a bag of women's articles: soaps, lotions, perfumes, makeup—the kinds of items scarcely found in Romania.

As the woman began to plow through our items and put them on the ground, Stela said, "I have something for you."

The guard snapped, "I don't want it!"

So, my wife kept the gift.

Every piece of clothing and all personal items were either on the table or floor. It was up to us to repack the suitcases.

Jeans were a valued piece of clothing in Romania, and we had fifteen pairs to give to seminary students in Bucharest. The female guard informed us only seven pair were allowed and took eight pair which she set aside on a stack of other items.

Stela explained we each had permission to bring in seven pairs, but the guard shook her head no. When my wife repacked the suitcases, she grabbed seven pairs back and hid them in her suitcase.

A little later, the guard walked over and looked at the pile as though she was trying to remember how many she had taken. She shrugged her shoulders and went on.

While one official asked Pastor Lawhon and me why we came to Romania, others focused on the car. I kept my mouth shut as they searched it until they started to remove the seats.

"Stop right there, boys. Anything you take apart or pull out, you'll have to replace—not me. This car isn't mine."

They had planned to pull off the door panels and yank the seats out. I knew there was nothing to find. Mercifully, they agreed.

Five hours later, Pastor Lawhon ran out of patience. He told me to translate.

"I have traveled all over this globe. Never have I experienced this type of treatment. I demand to know why you are doing this."

When the guard understood, he dropped what he was doing.

He asked, "Who is this man who travels all over the world?"

I explained to the guard Pastor Lawhon was one of nineteen leaders of an International organization.

The guard said, "I don't want to talk to him. I'm getting my superior."

He left and another guard came. He asked the same question. I again explained who Pastor Lawhon represented and the importance of his work.

This guard said, "I need to get my superior."

He, too, left and did not come back. Another appeared. Based on his uniform, he was an officer.

He spoke to us in English and asked us a few questions. Then, he ordered his men to put everything back into the car.

The officer turned back to us and began to speak English again. He then drew us about thirty feet away from the other guards.

He said to Pastor Lawhon, "Gentlemen, for two weeks you'll travel all over this country and yes, you'll be followed wherever you go."

At that point, I removed myself from the conversation. Later, Pastor Lawhon shared with me what the officer had said.

He said the officer told him, "When your visit is done, you'll go back to your country and live as free men. Just imagine what it would be like if you had to live the rest of your life in this country. How would you feel?"

I knew full well what it was like to live in the prison known as Romania.

At 6:00 AM they finally allowed us through the border. In the car, Pastor Lawhon, who stands 6'3" told me the officer's admonishment made him feel about two inches tall.

• • •

We enjoyed connecting with friends and family after a seven-year separation. Yet, we were saddened by the harsh reality their lives were worse than ever.

Our trip in Romania remained uneventful until our stay in Timisoara. We woke up to find our rear passenger window had been broken out. Apparently, the car's multi-paint job failed to convince people it was driven by gypsies. We taped cardboard to the hole and went on.

A few days later, we traveled to Bucharest. We visited a church where Pastor Lawhon spoke, and then we spent the night in a hotel. The next morning, we began our trip to Targu Mures.

The distance between the two cities is two hundred and thirteen miles. The dangerous, winding road took us eight thousand and seven hundred feet up into the Carpathian Mountains. We held our breath as the car hugged the curves.

Prior to getting to the mountains, miles down the highway, something did not feel right with the brakes. The brake pedal pushed too close to the floor board. I did not mention it; however, Pastor Lawhon, seated next to, me did.

"John, your brake light is flashing."

"I know."

His voice tensed, and he asked, "What's wrong? Don't you have brakes?"

"No, but we'll be fine. I'll drive slowly and use the emergency brake to get us to Targu Mures. My friend Stefan Poponut is a mechanic."

This was Romania, not the United States where there was a mechanic on every corner. Most towns in Romania did not have even one mechanic. It was already Monday, and in a couple of days we needed to leave for Germany to fly back to the States. I had to keep driving. No question a whole lot of prayers were lifted while I drove.

When we arrived in Targu Mures, I drove to Stephan's home.

I told him, "Something is wrong with the brakes. Can you check it, please?"

It did not take him long to find the problem. When he looked around the left front wheel, he called me over.

"John, come here."

He pointed to an area where fluid had been leaking. He pointed out another area on the brake line that showed some kind of tool had marked the line.

"John, this wouldn't happen even with a cheap car. Someone did this."

Because the valve was loose, it allowed brake fluid to be pumped out every time I used the brake. Someone had tampered with the valve which kept the pressure in the line. It was clear the Secret Police wanted us dead.

Stephan tightened the valve and refilled the brake reservoir. The brakes worked perfectly from then on.

Stela and I dropped Pastor Lawhon and his wife at the hotel. We had planned to meet for breakfast at ten o'clock the next morning. We drove to visit another pastor friend of ours for the night.

Of course, we knew this was illegal. No tourist or foreign visitor was allowed to stay in a Romanian's home. Visitors were required to stay in a hotel where they were watched and listened to.

My friend invited us, so we decided to stay with them. I was not under Romania's thumb anymore, so I was not afraid.

When we arrived, the pastor's wife said, "The head of the police called and asked for you to please come to their office tomorrow morning at 8:00 AM."

I was not surprised, since I knew the pastor's telephone was tapped. Fine by me, I was not concerned. We enjoyed our evening and I reported to the police the next morning.

When I arrived, there were two officers waiting for me. They escorted me, one in front and one behind me, down a hallway through some doors and into an office very familiar to me. It was the same office where Captain Hristea and I had our talks. I stepped into the room.

I said, "Man, how many times was I in this room? What a difference between then and now! Then I had to be careful what I said; now I can speak like a free man."

That seemed to set the officers back a bit from the surprised looks on their faces. We sat down at the table opposite each other.

One officer asked, "Mr. Muntean, we want to know how

you can have so much influence in the United States. What are you doing?"

I ignored the question and said, "You know my name, but I don't know yours. What are your names? Usually people know each other's names when they're conversing."

One of them answered, "That's not important."

I responded, "How sad that even at this level of authority, your names aren't important."

Of course I knew they would not tell me their names, but I wanted to make a point.

They ignored my comment and proceeded to ask me all sorts of questions about some Romanian pastors in California. I laughed at them.

"You couldn't make me an informer when I lived here in Romania. You really think I'd be willing to become one living in America? No way."

Sometime during my three-hour stay, they held up a ballpoint pen.

One officer asked, "Do you know what this is?"

I answered, "Of course, I do. I give it out to all my customers as advertising for my business."

I had no idea how they got it, except it made it clear I was still being watched and informed on in the States.

The interrogation returned to the question about my influence in the States.

"What kind of influence do you have to cause two senators from the United States to come to Targu Mures in 1984 and cause us trouble?"

I answered, "It's not important, but I'm glad they came because for six months after the church was demolished in Targu Mures, you wouldn't do anything for those people who needed a new location for services. When you heard the senators were coming, you resolved it in two weeks. I'm very glad I could do that."

The Ceausescu government was bulldozing churches, but making it nearly impossible for the purchase of new buildings for worship. In Bucharest alone, twenty-five churches, some three hundred years old, were demolished along with artifacts and priceless art. No amount of protest—from the people within Romania or the free world—stopped the destruction.

The officers continued to hammer at the question of my influence. I never confessed I had none at all. I had connected my local pastor friend with an American ministry which asked the senators to visit Targu Mures as they gathered information on the church demolitions. When I called my friend back to tell him about the senators, the Securitate listened in on the wiretap they had built into the big, black telephone.

"Everyone dies at some point in their life," the taller officer said.

The subject change startled me.

"Don't you feel bad your son, Johnny, is buried in Romania, but when you die you'll be buried in the U.S.?"

At that question something within me rose up, a strong urging. I began to preach to them.

"Either you're ignorant or want me to believe you are. In the Bible, it is clear when the trumpet of God is sounded the dead in Christ will rise, and then we, who are alive, will rise to meet

Him in the air."

It felt like I was in a pulpit. Their mouths dropped open. I continued several more minutes. They stared at me as though they were in a daze.

Finally, one of them said, "It's enough. It's enough."

· · ·

Pastor Lawhon who waited for us at the hotel with his wife had grown impatient.

Where were they?

Close to eleven o'clock, he called the home where we stayed and asked for me. My wife told him I had gone to the police station three hours prior and had not yet returned. Fearful I had been arrested Pastor Lawhon rushed out of the hotel and stormed into the tourist center, downtown.

"Where is John Muntean?" He demanded.

Wide-eyed, one employee answered, "We don't know."

The more than six-foot pastor slammed his fist on the table which made pencils and paper clips jump.

"If John Muntean is not back at my hotel by the time I get back there, I'll scream so loud they'll hear me in the free world."

At that, he turned and strode away.

Over in the municipal building, I was still being questioned when a woman ran into the room, out of breath, and pulled one of the officers from the room.

He returned and said, "There's an emergency! We need to let Mr. Muntean go, now."

They rushed me out of the building. The fear Pastor Lawhon

would carry out his threat was greater than their desire to interrogate and intimidate me. Within a few days we were back in Germany, heading for home.

• • •

Lieutenant General Ioan Mihai Pecepa, Ceausescu's right-hand man, the head of Romanian Intelligence wrote an exposé in which he revealed the horrific truth to the Western world regarding Nicolae and Elena Ceausescu, and their corrupt government leadership.

After defecting to the United States in 1978, he underwent plastic surgery to totally change his identity for his protection. His book, *Red Horizons*, was published in 1987, and was read over the airwaves in 1988. Chapter by chapter, through Radio Free Europe, Romanians heard the truth of their nation's Communist leadership for the first time in forty-three years.

In the preface of *Red Horizons,* Pacepa stated Ceausescu was nothing more than a "common criminal and assassin, who was up to his eyeballs in drug-trafficking, smuggling, theft, and the promotion of international terrorism. The Romanian people learned that the profits from these dirty deeds were being spent by Ceausescu and his family on a life of incredible luxury, while his citizens scraped by on the lowest standard of living in all of Europe."[10]

Pacepa reveals in *Red Horizons* that under Ceausescu, an estimated three hundred thousand Jews had been quietly redeemed and allowed to immigrate into Israel. Ethnic Germans ransomed to West Germany proved lucrative for the Ceausescus' personal bank account. The Communist leaders had made money hand over fist.

By the 1970s, monies ranged upwards to $250,000 American dollars per person, depending on their skills and expertise.

After hearing these disturbing truths, in late 1989, the people revolted. Hundreds died, but in the end they won freedom. The Ceausescu régime came to an end in December 1989 with the trial and execution by firing squad of Nicolae and Elena Ceausescu on Christmas day.

It was only then the world learned the truth: the beautiful, vibrant, and productive country once known as the Breadbasket of Europe had been destroyed by Socialist policies and total government control. In spite of all efforts to repair the damage, it can never be what it once was.

• • •

In its rush to get rid of evidence, the Securitate destroyed millions of documents. However, we were able to obtain several of the reports on us. We were shocked by how much we were watched before we left Romania and in the eight years up to the Revolution.

As we read the reports, it was clear informers will inform, but seldom is anything they report true. In order for officials to appear they were doing their jobs properly, a little truth and a lot of misinformation filled page after page.

In our case, Toma made it look like he was doing everything possible to get me to stop the hunger strike. In reality, he protected me.

The 1988 reports proved the most interesting details of all because they showed how desperately the secret police wanted to shut me up. The informer's lies from the States made it look as though I was spreading anti-government propaganda. The information was obviously not well-received in Romania.

The very last report after our visit in October 1988 covered a plan to stop us at the border. When it failed, they were apparently willing to try anything. They were willing to kill us if it came to that—a sobering thought. One report stunned me, if I was to believe what it implied.

The last day of our visit in Romania, a pastor friend invited the Lawhons, Stela, and me to visit them. We had a good time and discussed a number of things.

A couple years later I read the detailed report of our visit and every subject discussed; it seemed to show the pastor had informed on us.

Prior to another visit in 2004, I sent him a copy and asked him about it. He denied it then, and again, vehemently, during our face-to-face visit. Only recently did I realize it is highly probable the pastor's telephone had a microphone in it, and we had been recorded.

Once I had learned Pastor Pavel Bochianu, head of the Pentecostal Church of Romania was on the secret police payroll, I had gotten to a place where not too much shocked me anymore. To Pastor Bochianu's credit, I must say the Lord convicted him. He repented of his involvement and went to each person on whom he had reported to ask for forgiveness.

• • •

There is a saying in America: hindsight is 20/20. When we look back at our lives and our beloved Romania, it is powerfully evident God positioned people in high places to serve His purposes. He blessed my family and the city of Sighisoara through Comrade Danasan, municipal secretary of the Communist Party; Captain Soare, chief of the municipal police; and Major Toma, head of the Securitate.

Yes, they were all members of the Communist Party, but they were also Christians, and God used them for that time. There is no question of their arrest and imprisonment if their Christianity had been discovered. I am forever grateful for their part in our journey.

The suffering of the people in any city, town, or village depended on its leader's desire for power and promotion in the Communist Party leadership.

I must share one last story about Major Toma—about his character and love for Sighisoara and its people. At the time of the revolution in 1989, rioters gathered at the glass and ceramic factories which were close in proximity. Their intention was to go to the Fortress and destroy the Communist leadership offices.

Toma stood before them and said, "Fellow Romanians, please don't destroy your goods, your city. It belongs to you. I am with you."

The crowd believed him because he had earned their trust over the years, in spite of his position.

However, the leader of the people said, "If you're with us, then you'll go in front of us."

The determined crowd turned toward the Fortress on the hill, which housed the Communist Party offices. Toma, in front, led them as they walked through the main entrance into the yard. At that moment, the new municipal secretary of the Communist Party shouted from an upper window.

"Arrest all these people."

Toma turned and faced her.

"No, Madame Secretary, it's you who will be arrested."

That was exactly what he did. That day not only was a city was saved, but also lives. Not one window was broken.

Seven years after the Revolution, we visited Sighisoara. Toma invited us for dinner in his home. We enjoyed the evening and hearing the news it was someone in Communist leadership who informed Radio Free Europe everyday about my condition and progress during the hunger strike.

I do not want to give the impression there was nothing to fear in Sighisoara. Of course, there was. Other officials and informers were everywhere.

Yet, in my case, God's Word was proven repeatedly. He will make our enemies to be at peace with us and He will cause all things to work together for good.

These truths were a constant comfort to us in Romania. We have continued to see His truths in our beloved America.

CHAPTER 17

BLESSING FROM PERSECUTION

Blessed are you when men revile you, and persecute you,
and say all kinds of evil against you falsely, on account of Me.
—Matthew 5:11, NASB

THE MAN WHO HAS NO fear of death is a danger to the man
who or government which wants to control him. This was why
Christians filled the prisons in Romania. The hatred of Christians
by Communists affected every true believer, regardless of age.

This last story is not about me, but it must be told. It is a story
about what one of our current pastors experienced as a young man
in Romania. I not only admire him, but I am honored to call him
friend. I share his story to make a point.

At seventeen, Ovidiu Dorin Druhora loved the Lord. So much
so, his heart's desire was to become an Orthodox priest. He grew
up with the liturgy, the beauty of the cathedrals, and the statues and
icons. He loved the music, the solemnity, the reverence, and ritual.

He loved God. He was passionate. He also believed his church was the one true church. All others were wrong.

Nothing made him happier than the thought of a career in the priesthood. The reality of attending seminary was in jeopardy because of his crossed eyes. With only seven seats in the class and one hundred and fifty candidates, any reason to reject a candidate helped in the selection process.

Ovidiu sat next to his Pentecostal friend, Michael, at school where they had passionate debates about God, the gospel, and church. Ovidiu was so certain he was right, he promised when he became a priest, he would fight all the sectarian movements—the Pentecostals, evangelicals, and underground churches. He considered them all cults, and wanted to persecute them right out of existence.

As only friends with diametrically opposed viewpoints can do, they debated with great fervor.

One day, Michael said, "Even though you don't agree with what I'm saying, it would be good and wise for you to come with me. See for yourself."

Ovidiu agreed go with his friend. He was not prepared for what he saw or experienced when he joined five hundred worshipers packed into the house. They stood shoulder to shoulder and overflowed outside.

Never had he seen so many people attend a service. He was used to fifteen to twenty congregants in his church who participated in the services. Some people might come in and light a candle, and then leave.

However, these people prayed as though God was right in front of them. They had no prayer books. The music was filled with joy, and it was followed by preaching unlike anything he had ever heard. To this day, he remembers the subject.

The preacher taught from James 1:22–24 "But be doers of the word, and not merely hearers who deceive themselves. For if any are hearers of the word and not doers, they are like those who look at themselves in a mirror for they look at themselves and, on going away, immediately forget what they were like (NRSV).

Ovidiu experienced feelings he had never felt before. His world was rocked, his religious beliefs challenged. He found it hard to deny the reality of what he had witnessed—the passion for Christ, the sincerity, the simplicity, and the depth. Theirs was a world and form of worship totally foreign to him.

Back at school, he was torn all week between his attraction to what he experienced, and his need to reject it and stay with what he knew, what was familiar. He told a friend who happened to be a Baptist he wanted to go back to the city because he had gone to a Pentecostal service there the weekend before and wanted to go again.

The young man said, "Fine, I'm going there, anyway, to visit my girlfriend who is studying to be a nurse. We can go to our service in the evening."

Ovidiu agreed. They went to the morning Pentecostal service together, and then he took Ovidiu to a Charismatic meeting where his girlfriend awaited them.

The meeting was part of the Underground Church movement. About thirty people filled the room, mostly young adults between twenty and thirty years of age. It turned out some were Baptist, Reformed Lutheran, and Pentecostal. Others were Hungarians,

Germans, Romanians, and there were even a couple gypsies. Had they been discovered meeting together, they would have been arrested for anti-social activity and, most likely, imprisoned.

One person played a guitar and led the others in worship. Their faces glowed like they were angels. After a couple songs, the leader said he felt God say they should pray for Ovidiu.

Ovidiu was not certain it was God speaking to the leader. Outwardly he allowed it, yet inwardly he resisted. However, there, among those believers, on May 25, 1975, Ovidiu Dorin Druhora, met the Lamb of God, face-to-face.

No one, but Ovidiu can clearly communicate the power or beauty of his experience with the Lord. He said as he moved away from the glory of heaven back into darkness, he walked as though on a spiral staircase toward the bright light which shown down on the group of people who prayed around him. His new white robe gave off enough light for him to see where he stepped.

He journeyed through the darkness while cries of pain and suffering echoed and filled his ears. Never had Ovidiu been aware of such pain and agony.

Should I go there to help?

Surely, the light was certain to show him what to do. The world revealed a different dimension, one of pain, suffering, and lost souls—a world without God.

Two hours later when he came to himself, he sobbed and confessed his sins. He stood up from kneeling, and hugged everyone.

He cried, "I have seen the Lord. I have seen the Lord."

Ovidiu said he was out of his mind in love with Jesus, and filled with a deep desire to serve Him. Everything for him was about the

Lord and his desire to share this revelation with lost people. He called his parents, told his professors at the trade school, and he even stopped strangers on the streets.

The reality of Jesus was more real to him than the world around him. When cautioned by Michael and other believers, he answered, "How can I not tell people about Jesus? He's so real. I met Him. I experienced repentance and forgiveness."

Even now, Ovidiu smiles and admits he was a bit over the top in his zeal. Within the week, the persecution began at school. He had been a model student, had a scholarship, and wrote poetry which was published in the school paper. He had been a well-respected leader among his fellow students.

The school's diagnosis: he was crazy. They called his parents.

"Come quickly. Something is wrong with him. He's crazy, completely crazy."

His mother, a nurse, wanted to take him to the doctor.

He told her, "Mom, I'm okay. I'm not crazy. I'm coherent. Look at my grades."

In Ovidiu's classes, the professor said, "We hear you met Jesus."

"Yes, may I tell you about it?"

The professor agreed and let him go to the front of the class where he began to tell them about his experience with the Lord. He was only allowed to talk for so long before the professor interrupted.

"Stop right there. Instead of telling us the lesson, you spread Christian propaganda."

It never seemed to matter he had been prompted to share.

The Romanian grading system was on a scale of four to ten—ten being the highest.

Ovidiu was given a one. The grade did not exist, except for the direst offense. It represented an absence, too many absences, and a student was expelled.

While the school tried to deal with Ovidiu, he was evangelizing his schoolmates. First, were his dorm mates, and then he evangelized others. After lights out they gathered in the four-person dorm room, and held Bible studies and prayer meetings. They prayed for healings for each other. Very quickly forty young men shared Ovidiu's Bible and signed up for one hour per person.

When his parents were called, they tried to reason with him. They—not practicing Orthodox like he had been—did not understand why he risked losing his scholarship over religion.

The Securitate pulled him from class many times and told him to reveal who was responsible for this change. They wanted to know what the sectarians had done to him. They kept him for hours and questioned him about the evangelical cult.

When they told him they wanted answers, he said, "I'll be happy to tell you how I met Jesus."

He was often slapped for the statement.

Six weeks into his harassment, one of the school's assistant principals was assigned to meet with the new believers on a regular basis for re-education into the Socialist philosophy. They wanted to make an example of the Christians, so the first meeting was held in the auditorium.

The press was invited, along with city officials. One of the philosophy professors spoke. He explained centuries ago when man was not able to explain a phenomenon, he began to worship it and call it a god.

Ovidiu stood and challenged the professor.

"What you say is true about people who had no education, but would you be willing to open any page of the Bible, read a passage, and prove it's wrong?"

He was told to leave. When the meeting ended, he was called into the professor's office.

The professor then said, "I swear I'll do everything I can to get you expelled."

Ovidiu's answer was simple.

"No, no. I don't want to leave. None of us want to be misled. Just read a passage from the Bible, and if it's true, tell us why it's true. If it's not, tell us why it's not."

The re-education meetings were scheduled three to four times a week. After the first public assembly meeting, since there was so much chaos, many new believers became quiet about their belief, but a core group of fifteen remained.

When he met with them, the assistant principal, a quiet man, asked Ovidiu and the others to explain what they had been doing. He listened intently as Ovidiu shared his experience with Jesus. The young men told him about how they prayed, read the Bible, and about the songs they sang.

Over a period of two months, he grew increasingly curious. He asked for some of their songs. One of the boys brought a tape. Later, the man asked for a Bible. Ovidiu agreed to get one for him.

Then, he asked them to show him how they prayed. The boys knelt in a circle and began to pray for the assistant principal who had joined them on his knees. Sometimes, he asked the boys to sing a song or read a psalm. As far as the school officials knew, re-education was taking place in those three to four meetings a week, and it was: for the assistant principal.

The school day began at 5:00 AM every morning followed by an hour for study from six o'clock to seven o'clock in the students' respective classrooms. One morning at 6:00 AM, a student came into each classroom to tell the sectarians to report to the assistant principal's office.

Once inside his office, all fifteen believers stood in a line and wondered what was wrong. He looked at each one for a moment.

He then said, "Give me your meal ticket."

After he collected the tickets, he said, "No food for today. Today we're fasting, and at lunch time you're all to come here. We're going to pray for a friend of yours, Groza, who has terminal cancer. The doctors have performed two operations. They refuse to do a third because the tumor is all over his neck and throughout his body. He is dying, and we'll pray for him."

At noon, they met and prayed simple prayers. No shouting, praying in tongues, or anointing with oil, just simple prayers. The assistant principal prayed with them, though not out loud.

Within a couple days, Groza returned to school, completely healed. The assistant principal called Ovidiu to his office.

He said, "This is really serious. I'm considering giving my life to the Lord. What has happened cannot be denied. Groza is back in school with no sign of a tumor or any sickness."

When Ovidiu went home, he shared what had happened with his parents. He wanted to persuade his mother and father, who was also a professor, what he had experienced was real.

He argued he was not crazy, even the assistant principal of the school believed in the Lord.

Because of her desire to protect Ovidiu, from the crazy sectarians, his mother went to the Securitate and reported the assistant principal. He was arrested, put in handcuffs, and sent to prison for two and a half years.

Since the Romanian Constitution guaranteed religious freedom, the charges against the principal were: anti-social activity or anti-government propaganda. Ovidiu was interrogated and told the only reason he was not going to prison on the same charges was because he was a juvenile.

His relationship with his parents was tense. During the school breaks he went to the small prayer meeting in his village. His parents pulled him out, beat him, and locked him in his room. Ovidiu crawled out the window and went back. He was caught and punished again.

Finally, the believers in the prayer meeting asked him not to come because the meeting was illegal, and he put them in danger of discovery. Not understanding, he was hurt and felt betrayed.

Twice his mother kicked him out of their home, and the school had had enough. Finally, he was called to the chief principal's office. When he walked in, his parents awaited him.

The principal told him, "If you want to stay in school, you have to sign this paper. You'll be closely watched. You cannot talk about Jesus or God, you cannot have a Bible, hold prayer meetings, or do anything like that."

Ovidiu answered. "I'm not going to sign that. You can do whatever you want with me, but I'm not going to sign."

The principal explained, "This is what the Communist Party and secret police are giving me. I have no options. Sign and stay in school, or you're expelled."

Ovidiu refused to sign. His parents were shocked and humiliated. They did not know what to do. The official document of expulsion arrived during spring break. Ovidiu was guilty of anti-social activity.

Yet, he did not mind. A year of persecution by the school authorities had come to an end. No more searches through his personal belongings, confiscating his Bible, and taking his poetry. No more harassment, threats, and name-calling. No more being pulled from class and interrogated by the secret police.

His father was not home when the mail came. His mother screamed at him, shoved a few items of clothing in a plastic bag, and told him to get out.

"Go to your sectarian friends. Live with them. Don't come back here. You're no longer our son."

The opposition of Ovidiu's mother knew no bounds toward cults. When she saw any of his fellow-believers on the street in front of her house, she screamed and cursed at them from her window or door. Yet, she loved her son.

As before, she changed her mind and invited Ovidiu back into their home. That summer, she arranged to have the only television network in the country send a crew to do an interview with her family in order to expose all the sectarian's subversive activities and extremism.

Ovidiu's father was unaware his wife was involved. The team arrived on their doorstep with cameras and crew, as well as the municipal police and the Securitate.

As a young teacher, Ovidiu's father had been arrested because he refused to join the Communist Party. So, when they came to the door and wanted to do the interview, he would not let them inside.

"I don't care if you throw me in jail. I've been there already. You're not coming in."

They left, but not for long. The next day the municipal police came back. Ovidiu's parents were at work. The men demanded Ovidiu accompany them to the station. He refused to go with them, and said he would not go without his father. So, they took him by force.

When they arrived at the station, the television cameras were set up, ready to film. Despite the situation, Ovidiu felt an overwhelming sense of peace. The Lord spoke to his heart, and gave him one answer to any and every question he was asked: "You have been falsely informed."

Question after question rained down on his head. Where were the meetings held? What did the principal do? What did he say?

Ovidiu's answer remained the same.

"You have been falsely informed."

All day long, hour after hour, they asked and he answered. The television crew gave up.

"This is not working. We can't have a documentary of this."

The police tried different techniques, all kinds of promises, further schooling, high-position in the party; it went on and on. Then they turned him over to men who used physical force to get the answers. They beat him, yet his answer remained the same.

Furious at him, they began to beat him on his back and head with a chair until it broke. Still, Ovidiu refused to give them the answers they wanted.

All day long, the questions and beatings did not break him. The police then called his mother. They thought she may be able to persuade her son since she had arranged the Bucharest news crew to come for the interview.

It was to be a follow-up to her previous story about her search for her lost son which had run in the national paper. This time, she told how she saved him from the brainwashing sectarians. However, when she saw her son, beaten and bloody, she sobbed.

"My son, my son, look what I've done to you. It's my fault. I'm so sorry, so sorry."

The television crew peppered her with questions, but she refused to answer them. They badgered her, but the more they pushed her, the more hysterical she became. She continued to weep in deep sorrow and pulled her coat over her head, and then turned her face to the wall.

The journalists were relentless. In desperation, Ovidiu's mother picked up an ashtray and hurled it at the camera.

"No more, no more."

Ovidiu stood strong for his faith. Come what may, he refused to deny it.

• • •

Eventually, Ovidiu's rock-solid conviction won his mother over. She was the first family member to convert. Today, Associate Pastor Ovidiu Dorin Druhora and his wife are parents to five grown children. He is one of the pastors at Emanuel Romanian Church of God in Anaheim.

His life is proof—bearing up under suffering can bring glory to God. Ovidiu has lived this truth. Blessed are we when men revile and persecute us, and say all manner of evil against us falsely.

• • •

My four living children were my personal reason for the hunger strike. I was willing to die for their freedom, so they and their descendants never suffered as seventeen-year-old Ovidiu Dorin Druhora had suffered.

In America, a life without that kind of persecution is possible . . . for now.

THE HEART BEHIND
THE MESSAGE

For I will give you utterance and wisdom
which none of your opponents will be able to resist or refute.
—Luke 21:15, NASB

I CANNOT BEGIN TO EXPRESS what a joy and honor it has been to be a part of telling John's and Stela's story. Working through our language barrier was amazing and terrifically challenging. I do not know which of us experienced more difficulty interpreting the other.

We all thought it to be a good idea to give John a chance to share by including an interview. As we dialogued about his hope for the readers and motivation behind him telling his story, I realized our in-depth conversation—on a gut-honest level—was full of complication and nuances. It still did not translate well. However, I recognized John has answered questions for me, and revealed a little more every time as we talked through his story over the past year.

Recently, we discussed the questions he thought were most

important to answer, and then we rehashed his answers. I decided to unpack them a bit by sharing the deeper convictions I have learned from him in the process.

When I read the following statements back to John, he listened to, added, and revised them. We printed them out and he studied them to be certain. Ultimately, John Muntean gave his stamp of approval to the following answers. They may not be in his heart language, but they represent his heart:

John, why did you decide to tell your story?

At first, I wanted my grandchildren to know what it was like growing up in Romania, what we left behind to come to America, and why their freedom was so important to me. On top of that, for years our Romanian friends and family—as well as many of my customers—have encouraged me to write it.

They have said, "Americans need to know how this push toward socialism will affect America."

Socialism is the precursor to communism. In Romania, when the Communists came in, the Socialist agenda was immediately implemented. Once Communist total control was realized, the worst dictators the Romanian people had ever known emerged.

What would you say to the reader who might think you and your family did not suffer much because of your relationship with the Sighisoara officials and the amount of money you made?

My first thought is, God guided everything to go that way in preparation for the plan He had for me. Obviously, at the time I had no idea, but looking back it is clear to me. I have to give God the credit for the financial blessing, protection, and favor on my family and me while we were in Romania.

Rest assured, most Romanians in Sighisoara and across Romania did not have the same experience. Of course, part of my peace of mind was the fact the chief of police, Captain Soare, made it clear I did not have to worry about anything because it would not get pass him. God used him to protect me. Even with all that we still were not free, but were controlled by the communists. The children still suffered persecution in the schools.

How do you hope your book will affect readers?

I want readers to become aware of how God works in their lives and to trust Him and follow His lead. Secondly, through God's help, I want to see our country back to what it was when we arrived.

It might be hard for some readers to believe you were not afraid of dying during the hunger strike. What would you say to them?

I was not afraid. I was aware my life was in jeopardy from the hunger strike, but I never thought about it. We prayed and trusted God for success. He was the One who gave me the idea, so I trusted Him.

I understand you trusted God, you and Stela prayed, and you had faith. A reader might wonder if because Johnny died, you had no moments of doubt.

Yes, we prayed for Johnny to be healed, but we also prayed for God to keep him from being taken by the state. That was the most important aspect of our prayer. There was no way we were able to prevent them from removing him from our home.

We look at our prayer as being answered in two ways. First, his death meant the state could not ever take him. Second, Johnny actually received a perfect healing and was in the best place: heaven.

Had you lived in America do you think Johnny could have been helped?

No question about it. We were told there were operations which might have helped Johnny in America. I do not even know why the doctor mentioned it because we were in Romania with socialized medicine. They never would have allowed us to travel to America.

Do you have concerns about America under ObamaCare?

We had socialized medicine in Romania, under communism. They still have it, actually. It was corrupt and limited then, and it still is today. While we were in Romania, Stela needed an operation. The doctor was well-trained and did an excellent job. I had given him 1,200 Romanian lei and ten pounds of honey. Although paying the doctors extra was illegal, my wife's life hung in the balance. This was business as usual for Romanians. As with my father, we had no "extra" money to give the doctor. My father died.

On the second day, as he walked out of the room after giving me a full report on her condition, he turned and held up six fingers which let me know he wanted six hundred more lei. The amount—1,800 lei—was a month and a half of wages at the time. I did not judge him or resent his asking for money. He deserved it, but the system prevented him being paid enough to cover his expenses. I thanked God I was able to meet his request.

We visited some friends in Romania in 2006. Their mother, who suffered with diabetes, had already had her legs amputated to the knees. She was in the hospital in need of further amputation.

The doctor let it be known he needed 2,000 *euro* before he would operate. The family tried to borrow the money, but failed. No operation was performed, and the mother suffered from gangrene in her legs until she died in 2009.

There is no one who can convince me that kind of corruption will not happen under ObamaCare.

When the Soviets came in with their Socialist propaganda, why do you think 25 percent of the people welcomed it?

First of all, big-city Romanians who suffered under the Nazi occupation were ready for change. Five years of hunger and brutality had beaten the people down. Looking for anything easier, they were excited at the promise of six-hour work days, five days a week. They also believed the government's promises they would provide everything fairly and share equally.

Sound familiar?

Once strong Communist control was in place, it was not safe to complain the promises were nothing more than lies.

There is a true story I did not tell in the book about a man whose farm was part of the collective, yet he still had to work it. He was reported to have taken a few ears of corn off a stalk in his field. He was hungry, so he boiled the corn and ate it. The police came and arrested him for cheating the government of its portion.

The dumbfounded man said, "I don't understand. We were told everything was ours. I took from my property."

He was put in prison for that.

So, no one doubts me, I will share a personal story. The year before my father finally surrendered our land to the collective, he planted wheat not only in the fields, but up close to the house. The prior year, the government's quota had taken the entire yield. We had been left with nothing to take to the granary for milling into flour—we ate cornbread for the entire year. My father was determined to make every inch of land count.

Well, the wheat closest to the house ripened a few weeks earlier than the rest because it received the full sun. My father, mother, and I hand-picked the wheat and beat it on the floor of the summer kitchen to separate the kernels from the chaff. Once the threshing was complete, my father took it to the mill to be processed into flour for bread.

Someone who had seen us pick the wheat reported my father. He was ordered to appear at the police station in Valea Lunga, a village about ten miles from ours. Of course, since we had no horse or oxen to pull a wagon, he had to walk. He explained to the police chief why the wheat had been harvested earlier, and the family's need for bread flour.

God's favor rested on my father at the time; otherwise, he could have been arrested and sent to prison for cheating the government. We never knew how officials might respond. It was our version of Russian roulette. The police chief let him go.

Sometimes, they seemed to show arbitrary favor. Other times, they were exacting to the point of frustration. An example of this: up into the late 1950s, the officials inspected the gardens around people's houses to determine the government's quota.

This happened to my father-in-law. His large five-acre garden was filled with all kinds of vegetables including tomato and bell pepper plants. The government agent actually counted every tomato blossom and bell pepper bud.

My father-in-law asked, "What happens if the plants don't produce?"

He was told it was his problem. The government wanted its quota based on the number of blossoms.

Why do you think the collective system failed?

It has always failed, and millions of people have died because of it. The nature of many humans is not to do their share of the work, yet they want their share of the pie. Remember the landowner in my village who lost his farm to the collective? While he had offered incentives for the men to work, the fields were providing an abundant harvest. When it became part of the collective, the disillusioned men left it all to go to seed.

Was the right to personal property ownership not guaranteed in the Romanian Communist Constitution?

Yes, but so were freedom of religion and speech. How well did those work? They were only empty words on paper. I fear this is happening in America.

Let's talk about those for a moment: freedom of religion and freedom of speech.

Again, those liberties were simply an illusion for the free world. Any religious activity discovered, which did not come under the control and direction of the Ministry of Cults, was called anti-social activity.

Freedom of speech was also guaranteed, except for a whole list of forbidden anti-government speech. Anything some government entity interpreted to be anti-government was not protected. This included even talking about God or Christ. Forget about having a rally of protest by anyone similar to those is the United States. The only speeches and rallies were those organized by Communist officials where the people were required to clap and cheer as the speaker spouted propaganda and lies.

Sadly, Romanians were so conditioned by those experiences even now many have a difficult time clapping and cheering freely. The reality is we were always careful regarding what we talked about where others might overhear us. It might get us arrested.

I see it happening here in America. People in government leadership want to muzzle those who hold opposing views; particularly, some conservative talk show hosts. The government has enacted laws which muzzle what it calls: hate speech.

What about freedom of the press? Was it guaranteed?

Yes, as long as the press wrote positively about the government, its practices, and policies. Those journalists who did not, ended up in prison.

Should we be concerned with the push for more gun control and disarmament?

Absolutely. Never has a dictatorship or totalitarian government succeeded without the total disarming of the people. I made this point clear in my book. It was the first thing they did in Romania, demand all firearms be turned in.

A book by W. Cleon Skousen called *The Naked Communist* lists the forty-five goals to slowly, subtly take control of America and bring an end to our liberties as we know them. Here is an example.

Goal #3 reads: *Develop the illusion that total disarmament by the United States would be a demonstration of moral strength.*

In Romania, Marxist Communists took over the educational system within one year. Besides the indoctrination and persecution shared in the book, what were some of the other things students experienced?

The Christian students were not the only ones who experienced abusive treatment. If a non-Christian student did poorly or resisted indoctrination, they suffered mistreatment. Their parents' political views would be secretly investigated.

If a student had excellent enough grades to enter one of the trade schools, but the parents' beliefs displeased the Communists, the information might be used to keep the student out. It depended on the personal agenda of the Communist official in charge of school admittance.

Lenin and Stalin knew the value of winning the minds of the youth. Remember, Lenin said, "Give me four years to teach the children and the seed I have sown will never be uprooted."[11]

Earlier in the book, I mentioned Stalin's Young Pioneers. Beginning in the fifth grade, children were required to wear uniforms with red scarves. Everyone got the red tie, except any child with poor grades or those who were a behavior problem. The lack of red scarf separated them from the other students, effectively punishing and humiliating them.

I understand since the collective system failed, and laborers were hard to find, the government resorted to cheap labor during the harvest?

Yes, within a few years of taking over, the workers learned the truth: the government did not pay the promised wages. The government decided to use the students. All over Romania for the first three weeks of school, students from fifth to seventh grade were bussed from the school to the fields early in the morning to work into the late afternoon.

I, as a student; Stela; and my two oldest boys, twenty years later picked up the uprooted white potatoes. The government used prisoners and newly inducted Romanian soldiers for its labor force, as well. All of these used for forced labor never saw any of the benefits of their hard work. The best of the harvest was exported to other countries while Romanians went hungry.

Were other jobs mandated for the students?

Yes. Once a week we had to gather medicinal herbs, like chamomile and rosehips, which were dried, and then sent by the kilogram to the government to be exported. We also gathered leaves from a mulberry tree to feed to the silkworms which were kept in a special room in the school. Once the silkworms exited the cocoon and enough were gathered, they were shipped off to meet the school's quota set by the government.

What happened if a student did not do his or her part?

The student was given a couple of chances, but if the student continuously failed to collect his or her share, the student was expelled. It did not happen often, though, since parents wanted their children to be able to read and write.

Do you have concerns regarding the school system in the United States?

Very much so—I am shocked to see how cleverly some of the strategies of the Communist agenda have succeeded in our school system. For instance, Goal #17 states: *Get control of the schools. Use them as transmission belts for socialism and current Communist propaganda. Soften the curriculum. Get control of teachers' associations. Put the party line in textbooks.*

The text of our history books may change, but history is history. It does not change. This begs the question: why do today's history books tell a different story, especially regarding the founding of this nation, its founding fathers, and our Christian heritage? Clearly, it is because someone is putting a different spin on the story. That, by definition, is propaganda.

Goal #29 reads: *Discredit the American Constitution by calling it inadequate, old fashioned, out of step with modern needs, a hindrance to cooperation between nations on a world-wide basis.* This is what motivates the new spin. If Socialists can undermine that foundation of our government, then citizens will be more open to change and involvement in the international marketplace.

The list of Communist goals makes for chilling reading, especially when we see for ourselves how many of these goals have already been accomplished. The entire list is included at the end of this interview.

What is another goal which concerns you?

Goal #28 reads: *Eliminate prayer or any phase of religious expression in the schools on the ground that it violates the principle of "separation of church and state."*

In 1963, the Supreme Court of the United States ruled prayer in public schools was unconstitutional. Yet, today there seems to be no problem with schools allowing Muslim students time to pray. Teachers are being trained to accommodate students who practice Islam, which is being introduced in many ways into the American school system.

There is a push for Sharia law to supersede the United States Constitution in some of our court systems. Those in the Romanian Communist leadership twisted the law to accommodate their agenda, and the same thing is happening in America.

The enemies of America, within and without its borders, who believe in the Communist ideology and are implementing the forty-five goals, have done a thorough job.

The declining American morality is a definite concern for you. Tell me what you see.

Stalin said America could not be taken over by invasion or war; it would be done differently—promoting pornography, drugs, sex, drinking, rock and roll, and violence in movies. This is exactly what Goal #25 covers—destroying the culture through the media.

Many concerned parents, grandparents, pastors, conservatives, etcetera—who have seen the success of Goals #24 and #25 eliminate all laws governing obscenity by calling them "censorship", and a violation of free speech and free press—are trying to wake America up.

How does one define obscenity? If there are no absolutes, then there is no such thing. The Socialist/Progressives say morality cannot be legislated. The school system cultivates this mindset by refusing to teach right and wrong. Students are not taught to think for themselves, but rather, they are taught to parrot the party line. They are taught truth is relative. What's right for one person does not have to be what is right for another. There are several moral factors which concern me.

First, the traditional family is being undermined and falling apart because of it—proof Goal #40 works. It reads: *Discredit the family as an institution. Encourage promiscuity and easy divorce. Those who adhere to moral or faith-based standards for marriage are undermined—even vilified—in schools and society-at-large.*

Second, Goal #26 reads: *Present homosexuality, degeneracy and promiscuity as "normal, natural, and healthy." The success of the Socialists' effort has caused a breakdown in our society. School children, beginning in kindergarten, are being taught homosexuality is normal. Promiscuity is normal. Abstinence, however, is weird.*

High school students are given questionnaires regarding their sexual orientation and gender identification. In many schools, depending on grade level, all forms of sexual activity are explained in detail, so the young people are prepared to make wise sexual decisions.

All this is happening under the guise of preventing unwanted pregnancies and sexually-transmitted diseases. It seems teaching abstinence is the obvious choice. In most schools, however, it's not part of the agenda.

If a person does not want his or her head crushed, do not lie down in front of a train. Instead of encouraging students to stay out of dangerous situations, schools stay away from the topic of abstinence which dances too close to morality.

Most parents shake their heads thinking: how on earth did we get here? The stealthy indoctrination of our youth has been going on for decades. Unless students come from strong moral families, they have no moral compass.

Do you think the American public needs a warning?

I do, but I do not know if they will listen.

If they do not, what do you think will happen to America?

The same kind of destruction we experienced in Romania, but worse. The United States Constitution and Bill of Rights clearly lay out the role of government. They are the protocol for federal government leadership. Our founding fathers understood without these limitations of governmental power over its citizens, the result was tyranny or oligarchy.

Merriam-Webster's Collegiate Dictionary defines an oligarchy as "A small group of people having control of a country, organization, or institution. A state governed by such a group."[12] In New York City, Mayor Michael Bloomberg banned selling thirty-two ounce drinks. Fortunately, a judge declared it unconstitutional. The mentality behind this kind of power is the danger. For decades, America has been the frog in the pot of water on slow boil. No more.

If you had a message for the church, what would it be?

God's Word says, "and if My people who are called by My name, will humble themselves and pray, and seek My face and turn from their wicked ways, then I will hear from heaven, and will forgive their sin, and will heal their land" (2 Chronicles 7:14, NASB).

The future of America lies within the hearts and hands of Christians, yet, too many Christians have bought into the deception of Goal #27 which reads: *Infiltrate the churches and replace revealed religion with "social" religion. Discredit the Bible and emphasize the need for intellectual maturity which does not need a "religious crutch."*

The social gospel is superseding the Gospel of Jesus Christ in many churches. People believe they can pick and choose which parts of the Bible are relevant to their lives. The effects of their beliefs are rampant.

Divorce among Christians is higher than with non-Christians. Many Christian ministers stand in support of gay marriage. Some churches ordain lesbian and homosexual priests. There are pastors in the pulpit who confess they have lost their faith and have become atheists.

It is as if the churches of today each come up with their own standard, or plumb line. No wonder things are off-kilter.

First, the body of Christ needs to remember the Living Word is the plumb line God has given the church. Anything which does not line up with the truth of Christ is not acceptable. Then, those who are part of the body of Christ need to pray for America like we never have before—as one.

Jonathan Cahn said the same thing at the end of *The Harbinger.* We have got to take 2 Chronicles 7:14 seriously. It is our responsibility as the people of God.

I have another thing I want to say to the church.

What is that?

Many churches are run more like businesses rather than an

institution of ministry to those in need. It is up to Christ's followers to care for the needy and sick among us. Jesus said true religion is taking care of the widows and orphans.

Many decades ago, the government stepped in to offer its help. From that point forward, we can see how people have been seduced by free handouts. Goal #32 has already been widely implemented. Social agencies, welfare programs, and foster care—all of these outreaches which used to be at the heart of church ministries are now under government control.

People are addicted to the system. We ought to minister to the needy while pointing them to Christ.

That is a good point, John. If you could warn American Christians about three things, what would they be and why?

First, pastors and church leaders who have begun to use their own plumb lines *must* go back to believing the Word of God above all else. If the people who love God and trust Him will come together in unity and pray for our nation, God can save our country.

Second, Christian parents need to be careful about what schools their children attend and what they are being taught. They need to understand the school board's agenda. If they can home school, they should. If they cannot, at the very least, they need to do whatever they have to do to be the primary influence in their children's lives.

A few hours of church a week are not enough to undo the indoctrination happening in public schools. Attend school board meetings and do not be afraid to make a challenge when some part of a curriculum is dangerous.

Goal #41 attacks parental rights. Progressive politicians (neo-Socialists) are pushing for the House of Representatives to ratify the United Nations Convention on the Rights of the Child which gives a powerful foothold in eliminating the "suppressive influence of parents." Parents need to be aware of this, and God-fearing pastors need to challenge fathers to lead their families spiritually—to guard the hearts and minds of their children.

My last warning is this: we need to act like the church, not the world.

In 1954, Senator Lyndon Baines Johnson, wrote an amendment to a bill regarding 501(c)3 non-profits which kept non-profits from being able to endorse one political candidate over another. It effectively muzzled pastors in the pulpit.

For over two hundred years, pastors had been able to draw the clear line between right and wrong as taught in the Word of God. The congregation was encouraged to vote for the candidate who most espoused God's moral law. Now, however, too many pastors are afraid to speak the truth.

Truth is not relative, and it is non-negotiable. Pastors must not shy away from addressing the issues. How often are abortion and gay marriage the topic of a sermon?

So, you think pastors should speak out regarding moral issues, even if they become political issues, from the pulpit.

I absolutely do. People use the right to free speech to say all kinds of things in the public square. Rights of minority groups are protected, but Christians are forbidden or penalized because our core beliefs challenge progressive Socialist ideology—this sounds like a dictatorship, like the Communists in Romania.

How do you think Christians should speak about President Obama?

We are to speak the truth. 1 Timothy 2:1 urges us to pray for all our leaders and those in authority. God wants none to perish; however, that does not mean we cannot speak out when the leaders are clearly violating God's law and leading the country away from its heritage and greatness.

We should focus on the issues and be respectful of the office of the president rather than attack his character publicly. When President Obama is wrong, however, we should not be afraid to say so. Our nation was founded on Judeo-Christian principles. Never be afraid to speak the truth, but speak it in love.

Should the body of Christ always vote?

We need to vote according to God's moral law. When Christians vote for a candidate who supports abortion, gay marriage, as well as other issues harmful to the people and country, they align themselves with that spirit.

Voting is one of our most precious freedoms. We were forced to vote in Romania. We were presented with one candidate per position. If we did not vote, we were visited the next day by a party member and asked why we did not vote.

Americans must not take this liberty for granted. It is critical we vote for the candidate who will protect our freedoms outlined in the Constitution and Bill of Rights.

What else is necessary?

As Americans, we need to educate ourselves about what is going on. I have shared some of the goals of the Communist agenda for taking complete control in America because the list is so alarming and intentional.

So many goals have been successful to some degree:

- #15: Capture one or more of the political parties in the United States.
- #36: Infiltrate and gain control of more unions.
- #37: Infiltrate and gain control of big business.
- #38: Transfer some of the powers of arrest from the police to social agencies.
- #20: Infiltrate the press. Get control of book review assignments, editorial writing, and policy-making positions.

I share all this in hope well-intentioned citizens will do more. I encourage those who have just been living their lives, raising their families, working, and trying to make ends meet to determine to actively research the politics behind the new direction of our nation and act. This is about their children's future. Now, is not the time to be passive and disinterested.

Those who were disturbed by the film *Obama's America 2016* should find and watch *Agenda: Grinding Down America*. The two films go hand-in-hand to reveal the Socialist playbook.

What makes you proud to be an American?

I am proud and thankful to live in a country that allowed my family and me to live free, benefit from the opportunities provided, and live without fear of persecution. I was proud for what America represented when we arrived. I love America. I now fear for my country: America.

Is there anything that saddens you about being an American citizen?

Only the direction the country is headed. The United Nations is in our business. Google Agenda 21, and research the topic. It is being implemented in the towns, cities, and states across this land right under our noses. I guarantee America will not be the land of the free and the home of the brave any longer if every aspect of Agenda 21 is implemented. America and the liberties it has always stood for are in grave danger.

How are 350 million people deceived? Hitler said: "Make the lie big, make it simple, keep saying it, and eventually they'll believe it."

It is time to stop believing the lies, and start seeking the truth.

• • •

When we flew over New York Harbor on May 21, 1981, we saw the Statue of Liberty, her torch raised above the water. We had no idea what she represented. Today, however, we do.

Her plaque reads:

> Not like the brazen giant of Greek fame,
> With conquering limbs astride from land to land;
> Here at our sea-washed, sunset gates shall stand
> A mighty woman with a torch, whose flame
> Is the imprisoned lightning, and her name
> Mother of Exiles. From her beacon-hand
> Glows world-wide welcome; her mild eyes command
> The air-bridged harbor that twin cities frame.
> "Keep, ancient lands, your storied pomp!" cries she

With silent lips. "Give me your tired, your poor,
Your huddled masses yearning to breathe free,
The wretched refuse of your teeming shore.
Send these, the homeless, tempest-tossed to me,
I lift my lamp beside the golden door!"

She still lifts her lamp beside the golden door. She still welcomes immigrants in search of freedom from persecution who also seek opportunity. She stills helps immigrants like my family get on their feet.

America is the greatest country on the face of the earth. Not because of her many accomplishments, not because of her military force, not even because of her great productivity. America is great because of her citizens. They are the first to reach out and help, with money as well as goods.

Our Navy ships become hospitals for the wounded. Medical teams are quick to rush to areas of need. Volunteers from power and communication companies are quick to help. Faith-based ministries are often the first with food, water, clothing, and medical equipment.

The remains of American soldiers lie in cemeteries across Europe and other countries as monuments to America's willingness to fight for freedom for all.

Thousands of our combat veterans carry emotional and physical scars from their efforts to protect freedom—ours and other countries'.

Do some things need to change? Of course, they do. There are those within and without who want to bring America to her knees. There are those within and without who have an agenda of destruction. Yet, American citizens are strong. Our heritage of freedom ought not allow us to stand aside and let destruction happen.

If we, God's people, will fulfill our responsibility to God and our land, God will, indeed, hear from heaven and heal our land.

Thirty-two years ago, I feared for my children's and grandchildren's futures under a Communist dictatorship. I put my life on the line to gain freedom for my wife, my children, and me. Now, thirty-two years later, I again fear greatly for the freedom of my children, my grandchildren, and their descendants.

Please read the list of the 45 Communist Goals at the end of this book and see how many you can mark as accomplished. Then, you will see what needs to be done and where our hope lies.

Our only hope is in the promises of God.

Then you would trust, because there is hope; and you would look around and rest securely.
—*Job 11:18, NASB*

"Current Communist Goals" from *The Naked Communist*[13]

1. U.S. acceptance of coexistence as the only alternative to atomic war.

2. U.S. willingness to capitulate in preference to engaging in atomic war.

3. Develop the illusion that total disarmament by the United States would be a demonstration of moral strength.

4. Permit free trade between all nations regardless of Communist affiliation and regardless of whether or not items could be used for war.

5. Extension of long-term loans to Russia and Soviet Satellites.

6. Provide American aid to all nations regardless of Communist domination.

7. Grant recognition of Red China. Admission of Red China to the U.N.

8. Set up East and West Germany as separate states in spite of Khrushchev's promise in 1955 to settle the German question by free elections under supervision of the U.N.

9. Prolong the conferences to ban atomic tests because the U. S. has agreed to suspend tests as long as negotiations are in progress.

10. Allow all Soviet satellites individual representation in the U.N.

11. Promote the U.N. as the only hope for mankind. If its charter is rewritten, demand that it be set up as a one-world government with its own independent armed forces. (Some Communist leaders believe the world can be taken over as

easily by the U.N. as by Moscow. Sometimes these two centers compete with each other as they are now doing in the Congo.)

12. Resist any attempt to outlaw the Communist Party.

13. Do away with all loyalty oaths.

14. Continue giving Russia access to the U.S. Patent office.

15. Capture one or both of the political parties in the United States.

16. Use technical decisions of the courts to weaken basic American institutions by claiming their activities violate civil rights.

17. Get control of the schools. Use them as transmission belts for socialism and current Communist propaganda. Soften the curriculum. Get control of teachers' associations. Put the party line in textbooks.

18. Gain control of all student newspapers.

19. Use student riots to foment public protests against programs or organizations which are under Communist attack.

20. Infiltrate the press. Get control of book-review assignments, editorial writing, and policy-making positions.

21. Gain control of key positions in radio, TV, and motion pictures.

22. Continue discrediting American culture by degrading all forms of artistic expression. An American Communist cell was told to "eliminate all good sculpture from parks and buildings, substitute shapeless, awkward and meaningless forms."

23. Control art critics and directors of art museums. "Our plan

is to promote ugliness, repulsive meaningless art."

24. Eliminate all laws governing obscenity by calling them "censorship" and a violation of free speech and free press.

25. Break down cultural standards of morality by promoting pornography and obscenity in books, magazines, motion pictures, radio and TV.

26. Present homosexuality, degeneracy and promiscuity as "normal, natural, and healthy."

27. Infiltrate the churches and replace revealed religion with "social" religion. Discredit the Bible and emphasize the need for intellectual maturity which does not need a "religious crutch."

28. Eliminate prayer or any phase of religious expression in the schools on the ground that it violates the principle of "separation of church and state."

29. Discredit the American Constitution by calling it inadequate, old-fashioned, out of step with modern needs, a hindrance to cooperation between nations on a world-wide basis.

30. Discredit the American Founding fathers. Present them as selfish aristocrats who had no concern for the "common man."

31. Belittle all forms of American culture and discourage the teaching of American history on the ground that it was only a minor part of the "big picture." Give more emphasis to Russian history since the Communists took over.

32. Support any socialist movement to give centralized control over any part of the culture—education, social agencies,

welfare programs, mental health clinics, etc.

33. Eliminate all laws or procedures which interfere with the operation of the Communist apparatus.

34. Eliminate the House Committee on Un-American Activities.

35. Discredit and eventually dismantle the FBI.

36. Infiltrate and gain control of more unions.

37. Infiltrate and gain control of big business.

38. Transfer some of the powers of arrest from the police to social agencies. Treat all behavioral problems as psychiatric disorders which no one but psychiatrists can understand or treat.

39. Dominate the psychiatric profession and use mental health laws as a means of gaining coercive control over those who oppose Communist goals.

40. Discredit the family as an institution. Encourage promiscuity and easy divorce.

41. Emphasize the need to raise children away from the negative influence of parents. Attribute prejudices, mental blocks and retarding of children to suppressive influence of parents.

42. Create the impression that violence and insurrection are legitimate aspects of the American tradition; that students and special-interest groups should rise up and use "united force" to solve economic, political or social problems.

43. Overthrow all colonial governments before native populations are ready for self-government.

44. Internationalize the Panama Canal.

45. Repeal the Connally Reservation so the U.S. cannot prevent

the World Court from seizing jurisdiction over domestic problems. Give the World Court jurisdiction over nations and individuals alike.

EPILOGUE

MARCH 2013

IT HAS BEEN A LONG journey—not always easy, sometimes very dangerous, but a satisfying journey. My wife, Stela, and I will be celebrating forty-nine years of marriage. I knew God had blessed me with the right wife. She takes great care of me.

I still work fulltime with three employees, doing specialty work on vintage cars and boats. Stela brings me a fresh cooked meal every lunch hour. We live in the same home we purchased in Costa Mesa in 1985. Four year old, Toby, our Dachshund, not only protects us, but brings joy and laughter to us every day.

We are twice blessed by our church communities. We receive our main spiritual teaching from Emanuel Romanian Church of God in Anaheim with Pastor Lazar Gog, and occasionally are blessed to spend a Sunday evening at Free Chapel in Irvine with Pastor Jentezen Franklin.

It was my heart's desire to continue to live in a free nation which allowed our family true freedom of religion, and opportunity. What my children chose to do with this opportunity was up to them. I am proud to say, they did not waste their freedom or opportunity.

Three of our children live within a half hour drive, in different communities; our oldest, Ovidiu, lives in Portland, Oregon with his wife and three children.

Ovidiu married his wife, Adriana, over twenty years ago. He owns First Financial Mountain Mortgage, and Adriana has a realtor's license. She works in accounting at Providence Medical Center in Portland.

Their oldest daughter, Christina, attends the University of Oregon and currently is majoring in pre-law. She plans to switch it to pre-med.

Timothy, shares an apartment with his sister, Christina, in Eugene, Oregon and is currently getting his private and commercial pilot's license from Lane Aviation Academy. His hope is to join the military as a pilot.

Briana, a junior in high school, plans to pursue a career with the Federal Bureau of Investigation (FBI). She graduated from the Portland Oregon Police Junior Cadet Program in April 2013.

All three—Timothy, Christina, and Briana—are part of the Sunday night praise and worship team at East Hill Church in Gresham, Oregon.

Liviu, our second son, and his wife, Lilly, live in Corona,

California. Lee owns the very successful AAA Convertible & Sunroof in Costa Mesa. His wife works in a medical office as an administrator.

Our daughter, Tabita Cesario, lives with her two daughters in Fullerton, California. Tabita is a realtor with TNG Real Estate Consultants.

Her oldest daughter, Danielle, is a student at California State Polytechnic University (Cal Poly) in Pamona. Her major is hospitality and management—she loves event planning.

Karly, attends California State University at Fullerton. Her major is bio-science, and she is planning a career in radiology.

Our youngest son, Danny, lives with his wife, Ana, in Brea, California. They have four energetic, children—two girls and two boys. Danny works for Oaktree Capital in Los Angeles. Ana has a successful eBay business.

Their oldest child, Emily, talks about veterinary school for the moment. Elijah has decided to be a millionaire—when asked how, he says by saving money. Luke wants to race motorcycles and become famous. Three year old Giana has not quite decided, but as bright as she is, she will probably have it nailed by the time she is four.

• • •

I lived under a Communist dictatorship for thirty-six years. I have freely lived in America for thirty-two years. Daily, we face the reality our freedoms are being taken from us. We must stop it. If not now, when? If not us, who? If we do not, then what will the future hold for our children and grandchildren?

ENDNOTES

1 Richard Wurmbrand, *In God's Underground*, ed. Charles Foley (Bartlesville: Living Sacrifice Books, 2004), 23.

2 Ibid., 24.

3 Ibid., 60.

4 Richard Wurmbrand, *Tortured for Christ* (Bartlesville: Living Sacrifice Books, 1998), 34–35.

5 Ibid., 36.

6 Wurmbrand, *In God's Underground*, 31.

7 Wurmbrand, *Tortured for Christ*, 49–50.

8 Wurmbrand, *In God's Underground*, 270.

9 Ion Mihai Pacepa, *Red Horizons: The True Story of Nicolae and Elena Ceausescus' Crimes, Lifestyle, and Corruption* (Washington, D.C.: Regenery Publishing, 1990), 73–74.

10 Ibid., xiii–xvi

11 "Quotes by Vladimir Lenin" by Gordon State College, A State College in The University System of Georgia, http://www.gordonstate.edu/pt_faculty/jmallory/index_files/page0487.htm (accessed June 26, 2013)

12 *Merriam-Webster's Collegiate Dictionary*. 11th ed. (Springfield, MA: Merriam-Webster, 2003)

13 W. Cleon Skousen, "1963 Communist Goals for America" (extension of remarks presented by Hon. A.S. Herlong, Jr. of Florida in the House of Representatives, Washington, D. C., February 10, 1963) from The Naked Communist (Riverton: Ensign, 1960).

For more information about
John Muntean
&

Willing To Die
please visit:

Phone Numbers: 503-515-7199
949-226-1671
Website: www.willingtodiebook.com
Facebook: www.facebook.com/willingtodiebook
Twitter: twitter.com/Willing_to_Die

....

For more information about
AMBASSADOR INTERNATIONAL
please visit:

www.ambassador-international.com
@AmbassadorIntl
www.facebook.com/AmbassadorIntl